Musings from the Mountaintop

by
Bill Armstrong
...the Sage of Sedona

Copyright © 2006 by Bill Armstrong...the Sage of Sedona

Musings from the Mountaintop
by Bill Armstrong...the Sage of Sedona

Printed in the United States of America

ISBN 1-59781-910-7

All rights reserved solely by the author. The author guarantees all contents are original and do not infringe upon the legal rights of any other person or work. No part of this book may be reproduced in any form without the permission of the author. The views expressed in this book are not necessarily those of the publisher.

Unless otherwise indicated, Bible quotations are taken from the King James Version. Copyright © 1976 by Thomas Nelson Publishers.

www.xulonpress.com

Table of Contents

The Earth Walk	7
A Broken Doll	11
A Grandfather's Lament	15
An open letter to a person who has given up	19
A Tree Grows in Coventry	23
Beliefs That Matter	27
A Friendly Rattlesnake	31
Life as an Outsider	37
The Dreamcatcher	41
The Eighth Day	47
The Miracle of the Three Cacti	55
Motivation or Inspiration	59
The Bellringer	63
Ginger	69
The Tenth Wave	71
Living a Committed Life	75
Stained Glass Windows	85
Fences	89

Looking Up When You Can't Look Down 93
A peace prospective…from an old dove 97
Hopes and Dreams 103
A Good Cigar 107
The Storyteller 111
Managing Diversity 117
The Wall of Decisiveness 121
A Conversation with a Jackrabbit 129
Living Life in a Fishbowl 133
The Cookie Lady 137
The Gift of Spirituality 141
ATT-I-TUDE…or attitude? 147
The Eyes Have It 153
Discovering Your Inner-Person 157
Dealing with Feelings 161
The Burning Bush 165
The Cultivator or The Carpetbagger 169

Taking the Earth Walk

With the very first steps we take we begin a special journey that continues to the day we pass on to our final reward. It is the journey our Native American brothers and sisters refer to as 'the earth walk'. Most of us quickly recognize the great risk in taking that first step. We have held our breath when we saw a child wobbling in an attempt to walk…that first step was taken only after considerable effort. There were several awkward attempts and more than one failure before that first successful step was taken. And so it is for most of us as we begin our earth walk. We will experience a failure or two before we can move forward with confidence.

The significance of the earth walk is summarized in this anonymous quotation:

> **"If we look at the path, we do not see the sky. We are earth people on a spiritual journey to the stars. Our quest, our earth walk, is to look within, to know who we are, to see that we are connected**

to all things, that there is no separation, only in the mind."

The first line of the quote emphasizes the importance of looking up…of maintaining a positive perspective. When embarking on a journey to the stars it makes sense to keep your eyes focused on the heavens. Liberty Hyde Bailey, a noted Botanist and poet said it this way:

"One never makes the quest unless the mind is open at the start."

A journey, especially a journey related to matters of the spirit, is an exciting undertaking. It is never an easy journey, but each step leads to a new and deeper understanding of your inner-person and the potential value you can contribute to the Universe. Consider this thought offered by poet Bryant H. McGill:

"Join me in my quest for a greater understanding of our existence. Join me in my desire for a greater self. Join me as I seek the humility to love and understand my fellow man."

I believe this to be very important. So important, in fact, that when I conduct a workshop I ask participants to close their eyes for two minutes and listen to a Native American song entitled, "Who Am I?" The purpose of the exercise is to help each person to look inside him or herself and gain a glimpse of the inner-person. They are asked to look beyond past mistakes, failures, shortcomings, to ignore what other people say they see, and any self-limiting thoughts they harbor towards themselves. It is a good exercise, even though in that short span of time most people are not going to get a complete picture of their inner-person.

The primary benefit of such an exercise can be summarized in the words of spiritual leader and activist Mahatma Gandhi:

> **"In the attitude of silence the soul finds the path in a clear light, and what is elusive and deceptive resolves itself into crystal clearness. Our life is a long and arduous quest after Truth."**

Authors Richard J. Leider and David A. Shapiro made an excellent observation in their book, "Claiming your place at the fire". They wrote:

> **"By becoming better acquainted with our own story, we more fully understand the stories of others. We are freed from the perspective of seeing all reality as revolving around ourselves."**

This is a most important first step to making your earth walk...to be able to understand who you are and what you are expected to contribute to the Universe. In addition, it is important to realize that as an individual you are connected to all things... that there is no separation. We are all connected to one another. This is the purpose of our earth walk...to understand this connection and to make it even stronger.

In like manner a thin thread generally connects the 'musings' contained in this book. When reading some of them this thread will be obvious. In others the connection will be less obvious and will require more thought on your part. In any case I hope you will share the excitement and the growth of people who are experiencing their earth walk.

A Broken Doll

A few weeks ago I was walking down an old trail when I realized I had out walked my water supply and had become down right thirsty. Just ahead I saw an old cabin. It appeared it had long been deserted, but I knocked on the door anyway, more out of habit, I guess, than in anticipation of an actual response. Getting no response, I pushed the rickety door open and stepped inside.

The only occupant was a small doll left sprawled on an old couch. The doll was well worn. The dress was faded, one button-eye was hanging loosely by a thread, and an arm was missing. In bygone days one could have easily made one of several assumptions. Perhaps the little girl had outgrown the little plaything, or had gotten a new one to replace the old worn one. Maybe it had been abandoned. Maybe it had been carelessly forgotten in the preparations for the move.

But I'm almost ashamed to admit that in today's environment those weren't my first thoughts. Maybe it is the frequency of recent headlines and wire service stories, but my initial suppositions were more of a violent nature. Had a parent broken the doll in a fit of anger? Was it more a symbol of lost innocence...the child, through circumstances beyond her control, had found the doll less relevant in an age where children often have to grow up too soon? Was a kidnapping or abduction of some description involved...and the toy a casualty of a hasty departure?

It seems sad to me that the first thoughts at the sight of a broken or discarded toy are those of violence and anger. Are these initial thoughts just mine...the product of too many years of big city living? Would the thoughts been the same if I had seen the doll lying on a box of trash...or by the side of the road?

As I continued walking back to my home I thought a lot about that doll...that broken, abandoned little doll. It certainly wasn't because it was an expensive toy...at the most it probably only cost a few dollars when brand new. But for some strange reason the same scenarios continued to race randomly across my mind. How did the ragged little doll wind up alone in that deserted old cabin? Was a little girl...somewhere...grieving over a beloved toy? Had it merely become a casualty of her growing up? Had a newer, prettier doll taken its place? Was she an only child? The cabin was small and desolated...had the toy been her only companion throughout a lonely childhood.

But perhaps my greater concern was over my own cynicism. Why had I so quickly assumed that the broken doll had something to do with abuse...violence...and despair? Have I become so desensitized by the news headlines and the television sound bites that I could so easily gravitate to these negative and disturbing assumptions? Maybe I should pay less attention to those sensationalized headlines and stick to the sports section and the funnies. Maybe I should not watch so much television. Maybe there is something I could do as a concerned and caring human being to eliminate these terrible trends. Maybe this is something we all should be more concerned about.

    Maybe I wasn't as thirsty as I thought!

A Grandfather's Lament

Ah, there it is—my favorite fishing spot! A peaceful oasis in the midst of the cacophony I call "my world". It's perfect! Sun when I want sun...shade when there's too much sun. The stream flows swiftly by with the ever-present soft gurgling noises that have lulled me to sleep on many a summer's afternoon. And today there are an abundance of big white clouds to study. Best of all, although to many it might seem strange, the fish hardly ever bite. That's right! In the eight years I've been coming here I bet I haven't caught a dozen fish...and those I threw back in. They are interruptions to the relaxation I otherwise enjoy. I wouldn't even bait my hook, except it seems downright dishonest to come here and not at least <u>try</u> to catch something. I guess I like this place more for the <u>thoughts</u> I catch than the fish.

Doggone it's quiet here! And look at those clouds! Today the clouds are especially magnificent...sometimes I think they actually talk to me. They speak of mysterious things...things I might miss on a regular day. I lean back on a big tree and shade my eyes for a better look. Let's see...that one looks like a car...and there, a dog with a tiny little tail. Over there...that looks like an old man, all bent over and walking with a cane...he looks so lonely! It could be me in a few years...well not for a long while, I hope. I mean, I'm not <u>real</u> old... and I don't need a cane...heck, I'm still in my prime...well, almost. But I am a grandfather.

You know it's funny how times have changed. I can clearly remember my grandfathers and the influence they had over my life, and yet they both died when I was a young boy. They weren't rich men...or educated...or spectacular in any way. And yet I loved those men. One lived close by and I saw him several times a week. The other lived in another state, but I saw him, oh, probably once a month, or so. As a boy I looked forward to seeing them...spending time with them...listening to their stories...and their advice. I was proud when they took time to counsel me, and to share their experiences. I reveled in their stories of the old days and how they struggled to overcome difficulties. I saw them as a resource...a source of knowledge...a reference point to use as adulthood came ever so slowly to my door. They were real men in every sense of the word, and even today I think about them often as I struggle along the pathway called Life.

How times have changed. Now I am a grandfather. I am an educated person...I have advised some of the titans of industry... I have earned respect in boardrooms across the country...I have walked onto platforms and had thousands of people listening to my words. And yet, as a grandfather I have been somewhat of a bust!

My grandchildren do not clamor to be near me...or to hear my words. My advice and suggestions do not get the pretense of a responsive ear. Why? What have I done that has earned me this reaction? Is it the times we live in? Is it the fact that great distances separate us? Is it television...or Nintendo...or the fact that today grandfathers are frequently stereotyped as crabby, old men who lecture and criticize young people? Probably all of the above!

The young people on television today are often flip know-it-alls who have no respect for age, or much else for that matter. They seem incapable of accepting anyone's advice...let alone from an old codger who is the butt of a thousand jokes. Then, too, we are a transient society. We don't live in the same cities anymore. My closest grandchildren live nearly four hours away. Between my travel schedule and their activities, I'm lucky if I see them once or twice a year. I can offer no inputs into their lives...nor am I ever asked for any. I am concerned that they will miss out on the experiences I have had learning about how to overcome adversity...that sacrifice and hard times are a normal part of one's life, to be faced head on—not to be blamed on others. They need to know that we are responsible for our own mistakes...that government is not meant to handle all of our problems and to provide a balm for every ache. They need to know that real love is a priceless commodity and not something that happens in the back seat of a car. No...wait a minute...my grandfathers never gave me that advice! I found that out much later!

Anyway, maybe it's not too late. Maybe I'll go home and give my grandchildren a call. Better yet, I think I'll write them a long letter. That way maybe they'll save it and read it later when they can better appreciate the message. I'll tell them I love them, and how I miss them. That will be a good start. Maybe I'll get a chance to offer advice...later.

Yeah, I never catch any fish here...but occasionally I catch a good idea.

An open letter…to the person who has given up on Life:

Dear Friend:

This day to you must seem like a very bleak and dismal day. It must seem as though your entire existence is without meaning and purpose…that taking one more step along the pathway of Life would be just too difficult a task to bear. You feel that Life has nothing left for you…no more opportunities to experience success and happiness. Well, friend I'm writing you this letter to tell you that there is a bright future ahead…an important future…a meaningful future. Please let me explain.

As a newborn soul, when you were first released into the Universe; you made a bargain with the Creator to fulfill some specific task, or series of tasks. This was a binding contract made directly with your Creator. It may not have been a lofty task, or a difficult task like those agreed to by people such as Mahatma Gandhi, or Mother Teresa, or Michaelangelo. You probably did not agree to bring about world peace…feed the starving masses…or create a masterpiece.

Your task may have been a relatively simple one...to befriend a lonely person...to right a wrong...to provide guidance in a time of crisis to another person. You may have agreed to accomplish some seemingly small and insignificant task. Maybe even a thankless task. But regardless, it was something you agreed to do. Something the Creator saw as sufficiently important to create you as the only person with the capability to see that particular task through to a proper conclusion.

So no matter how bleak Life may seem to you at this point in time, you probably still have that task...your life's Purpose...to fulfill. To walk away without having accomplished that task would be wrong. You owe it to yourself...to everything you have stood for...to spend your allotted time seeking out your Purpose and achieving it. Consider this thought from Marian Wright Edelman:

"Whoever said anyone has a right to give up."

Only the Creator has the right to determine the length of your stay on this Earth. This is not a decision for you as an individual to make.

Consider this thought as well...

Yesterday is history, Tomorrow is a mystery, Today is a gift from God...that is why it is called "The PRESENT."

There is a great deal of truth in this little piece of wisdom. Each day is a gift. It is a gift for you to enjoy. A gift for you to use, in whatever way you choose. And let me assure you of something else. You were not placed in the Universe to fail! As long as you do not quit you cannot fail! It is part of the agreement you made with the Creator. You will certainly experience a failure or two along your journey, but that is just part of the learning process.

So I say to you...as a friend...don't be hasty. There **IS** another way! There **IS** an alternative path to take. Look hard...it is there for you. Listen to the still, small voice that comes to you in the cry of a bird...a soft breeze...a raindrop. It will be your message from the Creator. A message of hope, and love, and renewal. It is there for you.

Remember the words of Albert Schweitzer:

> **"In everyone's life, at some time, our inner fire goes out. It is then burst into flame by an encounter with another human being. We should all be thankful for those people who rekindle the inner spirit."**

There are many people whose Purpose in life is to help you. Be aware of that and when you encounter them let them help you in whatever way they can. Leah Maggie Garfield wrote in her book, "Angels and Companions in Spirit":

"None of us is alone; it is not permitted...the Holy Spirit has a multitude of emissaries whom we refer to as 'guardian angels'. Many times a so-called guardian angel is in fact a lifetime guide."

Look through the darkness that surrounds you at this moment in your life to find the light that lies just ahead of you.

God bless you...Friend.

A Tree Grows in Coventry

A tree was planted today in Coventry. No bands played. No crowds gathered. No plaque was laid to mark the event. Just a small boy came…alone. He dug a hole in the soft brown earth. Ever so gently he set a seedling into the hole. He stepped back a few paces to make certain it was standing straight. Then he patted the soil firmly around the roots. A pail of water from the nearby stream was carefully poured over the fresh mound of dirt. He stood for a long time admiring his work. It wasn't a major undertaking…it only took a few minutes of his time. But somehow he knew that what he had done was significant…at least to him.

As he stood there he silently shared his thoughts with the tiny seedling. He shared his dreams…plans that were barely in the early stages of conceptualization…but dreams nevertheless.

A tree grows in Coventry. A young man as straight and sturdy as the young tree itself stopped by for a time. He was going away to war. His future was uncertain, and it just seemed proper that he visit his tree before he left. He thought again of the dreams he had shared with the seedling years ago. He still had the dreams...they had taken form and had grown since that day, just as the tree had grown and sent its branches toward the sun.

But the young man knew that now...at least for a little while...his dreams would be on hold. A war was being fought far away, in a land he only knew from books. His country needed him to join thousands of other young men to help bring an end to the fighting. He knelt for awhile, sharing his concerns with his tree. He wasn't sure he would ever see his tree again...so he took his time. He let his eyes roam up the trunk over each branch. The tree had become his silent companion, and he wanted to remember it in every detail. Then he stood, and after one last look, he turned and walked back down the road.

A tree grows in Coventry. Today the young man came back, this time he had a young woman with him. He showed her his tree. By now it was even taller; its branches spread wide in all directions. He told her of the day the seedling was first planted...and of the dreams he had then. He told her how his dreams had grown along with the tree. He shared with her his dreams for the future. And then he asked her to be a part of them...he asked her to marry him.

A tree grows in Coventry. Today the young man and woman returned to the tree. This time they brought a small group of people with them...a minister...a few friends. Today they pledged to share a lifetime together. They made promises in front of the tree. Promises that they would share each other's dreams. That they would live together in times of plenty and in times of need...in sickness and in health. That they would nurture their love and allow it to grow... just as the boy had done with the seedling, so many years earlier. Today in front of that stately tree the young couple were united in marriage...and everyone shared in their joy.

A tree grows in Coventry. Today the young couple returned to visit the tree. But they brought with them a little boy...their son. As they sat beneath the branches the father shared the story of how the little seedling had grown into a mighty tree. He told his son about his dreams, and how through hard work and determination, they had been achieved. Then the young couple took the little boy's hand, and they told how much they loved him. They encouraged him to dream his own dreams...and they promised to give him their encouragement and support. Then the three of them dug a little hole in the soft brown earth. They gently placed a seedling into the hole. They stepped back a few paces to make certain it was straight. Together they patted the soil around the roots...and gave it water from the nearby stream.

And now two trees grow in Coventry.

Beliefs That Matter

When I was a young boy, the old minister at our little church gave a sermon that, for some reason, still sticks in my mind. The title, "Beliefs That Matter", primarily addressed beliefs of a spiritual nature that could have an impact on a person's life. The message was a simple one, but it is one that continues to remind me of the importance of our beliefs and their role in our daily lives. You see, we tend to become committed to the things we believe in. The message, in spite of its simplicity, has many applications.

Of all the things we believe in...or <u>think</u> we believe in...which really matter? Which beliefs are important enough to commit to...to build a life upon? So often we do not give this much thought.

If you do not believe in <u>something</u> the chances are your life will slip by and you will never glean a full measure from the effort you put forth. You will find your efforts have been dissipated across a broad spectrum of possibilities, without making the impact you may have intended. There are many areas upon which we as individuals might choose to focus our attention. As a leader there are several areas where you can make a significant contribution:

Believe in your organization. Too often today our leaders are not managing to _win_. Rather they manage to avoid losing! Many organizations are being managed in a "prevent defense". Aggressiveness is set aside in favor of maintaining the present position...the status quo. This strategy rarely works! It doesn't work very often in sports...it doesn't work very often in business. Believe in your organization enough to sustain aggressive growth. In today's economy an organization that aspires only to hold on to what it has will soon be swept away by a competitor that can respond more quickly to changes in the marketplace.

Believe in your people. Over the years I have heard any number of CEOs stand at company dinners or picnics and tell their employees how important they were. They would say something like, "If all our buildings were to burn to the ground, and I still had all of you, I could begin again and rebuild the company!"

It was a nice sentiment and seemed to be appreciated by most employees. But today it seems that some of our organizations...make that _many_ of our organizations...have lost sight of the fact that it IS the employees that make the wheels turn.

To grow your organization it is important to once more recognize the value of your people and the role they play in your success. A lack of confidence is one of the major contributors that limit a person's growth. By increasing their confidence you will greatly enhance their value as an employee. Invest in training. Help them learn new skills that will make your organization even stronger. In return they will continue to add value to the organization.

Believe in yourself. As the leader you must believe in yourself, and in your ability to build a strong, flexible organization. I'm not talking about "ego". I am referring to self-esteem. Ego tends to block your view of all of the available options. It may even cause you to make decisions that are less than optimal. It may interfere with your personal relationships...at home as well as at work. Recognize the importance of your position as a positive role model and leader.

Believe in yourself...make a difference!

And thank you, Reverend Lemmon, for reminding us that our beliefs do matter!

A Friendly Rattlesnake

I was sitting on my favorite writing rock looking to the heavens for some divine inspiration, when I saw a rattlesnake slithering toward me. He was within ten feet of me. Slowly I reached for the stout walking stick I use when I hike. I raised it above my head when, to my surprise, the snake spoke. His voice was raspy, but I could hear him clearly.

"Are you going to try to kill me?" he asked.

"Are you going to try to kill <u>me</u>?" I asked cautiously.

"I don't know…are you a peaceful person?"

"I like to think so."

"Have you ever killed one of us before?"

"Yeah, many years ago."

"Why?"

"To be truthful, it seemed like a good idea at the time."

"Have you ever eaten one of us?"

I hesitated. I admit this conversation was making me a bit uneasy. I wasn't quite sure how to respond.

"Well, have you?" He asked rather impatiently.

"Okay, I've had a rattlesnake steak once…and some soup that was supposedly made from rattlesnake meat."

"Did you like it?"

"It was okay, I guess."

"I've bitten humans a couple of times. Can't say I enjoyed it… too bland for my taste."

I was getting the impression he was putting me on.

"From what I hear you and your buddies have bitten quite a few of us!"

"Well, you humans won't leave us alone. You keep invading our space. Everywhere we turn you are building a bunch of new homes or a ranch or something. Heck, they're putting up a Wal Mart and a Starbucks in my old neighborhood!" He paused. "Actually we are a rather pleasant and peaceful lot."

I had to chuckle.

"I haven't seen or read any evidence of that."

"Well it's true…don't we always give you a warning when you get too close?"

"That's what I've been led to believe."

"Some of my cousins don't even do that! You won't get a warning from a water moccasin or a fer de lance!"

I shrugged. "Okay, I'll give you that."

"Your kind even catch us for sport. In several states they even have festivals where they catch and make sport of us...even eat us as a delicacy!"

"So I've heard. But in some areas you are worshiped in churches."

"Yeah, and I hear that's a real picnic! One of my friends claims he was caught for some kind of a church service. He said some toothless old guy with tobacco breath was actually kissing him. He said he was terrified. He only got away by the skin of his fangs!"

I looked at him in disbelief.

"That was a joke!"

"You're a regular coiled-up comic!"

"You seem surprised that we could have a sense of humor."

"I am...I truly am."

"Well it isn't easy nowadays...we have a lot of gripes."

"What gripes?"

"Well for one thing it is not a great deal of fun to have to crawl on our bellies all the time. After all, that curse was put on all of us thousands of years ago...none of _us_ ever talked anyone into eating an apple. None of us have spoken to a single human being since that day. I mean, you try to be friendly to someone and look what happens. You call that fair? Over the years a lot of us settled in Ireland...then that Catholic guy chases us out of the country!"

"You mean Saint Patrick?"

"To you he might be a saint, but to us he's a terrorist!"

"When you put it that way... By the way, do you have a name?"

"Elmer...my given name is Elmer."

"Elmer? That's a strange name for a snake."

He became somewhat defensive.

"What do you mean...strange? How many snakes have you ever met?"

"Very few, actually. But..."

"I happen to like my name!"

"Sorry...you're right. It's perfectly fine name."

I thought this was a good time to try to change the subject.

"I've always been curious...how do you tell the difference between male and female snakes? I mean it is fairly easy to tell the difference between male and female birds...actually that's true for most species. But snakes usually look alike."

"We have the same problems with human beings. To us you all look alike."

I had to laugh. "Touché!"

"Don't you ever get confused?"

"I've got to admit I do get confused occasionally. It is hard to be sure sometimes... especially at a distance."

"Same here. Every so often I make a mistake as well."

"Embarrassing...isn't it?"

"It can be...female snakes can be moody at times. Although they can be real sweet during the mating season."

"Hmmm...that must be true of most species."

"That's why I stay single!"

"I don't know…being married can be a wonderful experience, if you find the right one."

"I'll take your word for it, but for me I'm happy with things as they are."

"Speaking of family…I see it getting dark. I better head for home."

"Yeah, I'm getting hungry…I better go catch a mole for dinner."

"Well, Elmer, I've enjoyed talking to you. Maybe we will meet again sometime."

"Maybe…just be careful you don't step on me."

"I can promise you I will continue to look out for you and all of your friends!"

"That's always a good idea. When someone steps on us we tend to get 'rattled'. We've been known to have a 'hissy fit'."

"Very funny…see you later, Elmer."

He turned and waved his rattle. Then he slithered down the path. I never saw Elmer again, but I'm sure he is around these parts somewhere. I guess he knows where I am if he ever wants to stop by.

Dear Reader:

I should point out at this juncture that most everything you will read in this book is the absolute truth. Occasionally I might take a brief flight of whimsy. This <u>could</u> be one of those times. I won't say for sure. However I would caution you that if you happen to run into a rattlesnake here in Arizona, or anywhere else for that matter, be wary. Say to that snake in a loud voice, "Hey Elmer, is that you." If that snake doesn't stop in its track and respond to you...you are on your own!

Life as an Outsider

There have been many times in my life when I was convinced I was an outsider...a person who didn't belong in the time-space I was occupying. Had I been deposited here by an alien spaceship, and been forgotten? Was I born from a one-of-a-kind seed that had floated here from some faraway place? I knew I was different, but I was not quite sure how or why. It was a challenge to adapt. Most of the time I did...almost. It was as if I were a piece of a jigsaw puzzle that didn't quite fit...or rather, like I was the left-over piece when the puzzle had been completed. Somehow a vital part in humanity's grand scheme, but where? How? Life was almost like an out-of-body experience. I walked and talked with those around me, but I was always just a bit detached...always searching for my special place.

I went to school, made friends, grew up...but always just a tad out of step with the others. Never especially adept at sports...never a great student, I plodded through my early years. I developed the habit of taking shortcuts...just enough to get by. Never pushing hard enough to excel at anything... and yet maintaining an above average position at everything I attempted.

I was a loner, in a way...yet surrounded with family, friends, and acquaintances. I know myself better than anyone else, but who am I?

Still I searched.

Family life was normal, I guess. Close...but detached. Love and respect came much, much later. Social life was more difficult. While it was easy to make friends, I never had that 'special' friend, the kind with whom you share a special bond throughout life.

I never quite fit in at school. I had my share of teachers who nurtured me and helped me collect the potpourri of information, useful and otherwise, that fills my head. I also had a few who added to my confusion and whittled away at my self-esteem.

My spiritual life has also been a challenge. Throughout my life I have looked for God in many places. I searched in different religions, from the traditional to the less orthodox...formal and less formal. In each case I caught a brief glimpse of divinity, but never the complete fulfillment I was seeking. On my journey I have met men and women who I felt were excellent examples of the spiritual model I was seeking. I also found people, often in leadership positions, that exemplified the absolute worst of spiritual models. I found that confusing... so I continued searching. Then, much later, I found Him in the privacy and solitude of prayer. I learned one thing that stands out above everything else...<u>every</u> <u>prayer</u> **IS** <u>answered</u>! No word offered up in sincere and earnest prayer ever escapes the ears of the Supreme One...the God of all Gods. They are heard <u>and</u> answered, but in His time and in His own way. The trick is to be open-minded enough to recognize <u>WHEN</u> it is answered and <u>HOW</u> it is answered! Rarely does the answer meet our <u>precise</u> expectations. But it is always the <u>right</u> answer...even though in our limited range of vision it may not seem to be. A great part of any spiritual journey is acquiring the ability to recognize, and accept, this fact.

I have also learned that I am <u>not</u> a mistake or aberration of some sort. For some reason this is the way God intended me to be. I was placed on this earth, at this point in time, with a specific mission. I have some role to play that is both important and meaningful...it is up to me to find it...and accomplish it! Only I can complete <u>my</u> mission! I can, and will, get help along the way...but completing <u>my</u> mission is <u>my</u> responsibility! No one else, no matter how well intended, can fulfill it for me. It is mine alone...mine.

...and still I search.

There have been times when I thought I had caught a glimpse of my 'place' in life, and I was filled with unbridled joy. When I realized it was an illusion...a mirage...I felt depressed. But I realize that neither emotion can completely overwhelm me, for I am resilient. I am flexible...I can bend with the strong currents that each of us encounters throughout the life-journey. As St. Paul told the Philippians:

"I know both how to be abased, and I know how to abound: everywhere and in all things I am

instructed both to be full and to be hungry, both to abound and to suffer need."

And so my search continues. Each day a few steps forward... some days, a step or two backward. But no matter, I will never stop until my journey is complete. Perhaps some day you and I will meet as we make our earth walk ...together.

The Dreamcatcher

Since my first visit to the Southwest I had been intrigued by the 'dreamcatcher'. It can best be described as a hoop containing a small hole surrounded by a spider-like web. It may be plain or ornate... large or small. According to the legend, Native Americans believe the air is filled with both good and bad dreams. Traditionally a dreamcatcher is hung in the home, or on a baby's cradle. It is believed that the good dreams pass through the center hole to the sleeping person, while the bad dreams become entangled in the web and die in the light of the dawn. In the words of recording artist Nana Raven:

> "I'll let your good dreams pass on through
> But bad dreams all I'll catch for you.
> I'll hold them tight till morning light
> Then let those bad dreams all take flight."

I had decided to buy one for my office, but could not find one that was just the perfect size for the wall across the room from the spot where I am most creative. As we were heading for the airport I was suddenly overcome by the desire to buy one before we left.

By the side of the road, sheltered beneath a grove of shade trees, we came upon a group of Native-Americans displaying their wares. For the most part they were the usual items...pottery, turquoise and silver jewelry, leather goods, etc. Some were handmade...some were imported imitations. Most were similar to the trinkets for sale everywhere in the southwest.

I was attracted to a display that included a few dreamcatchers. The table was attended by a plump young woman, perhaps in her mid-twenties. A chubby little baby was at her side. The child's laughter seemed to be infectious. Most of the people seemed happy even though business was slow. In the background a large, elderly woman sat in a shabby overstuffed chair next to a rusting trailer.

As I inquired about the price of a small dreamcatcher the old woman's eyes opened wide. She sat upright and began staring at me. After several moments she stood up and pulled a brown paper bag from beneath her chair. Then she slowly shuffled over to where I was standing. Waving her hand to get my attention she spoke briefly in Navajo to the young woman. The young woman turned toward me with a puzzled look on her face.

"Is something wrong?" I asked.

The young woman shook her head. There was a brief, but animated exchange between the women. The younger woman shook her head in protest, but the older woman was adamant. Finally, with a shrug the young woman turned to me.

"My grandmother says you should have a special dreamcatcher she has made just for you."

"She made it for me?" I responded. "But I've never seen her before."

The young woman shrugged helplessly as the old woman pulled a large dreamcatcher from the paper bag and thrust it toward me. I took a full step backward, expecting it was some sort of a come-on. But again the old woman thrust the dreamcatcher toward me. The young woman shook her head in disbelief. "She insists it was made for you."

I hesitated as if taking possession of the dreamcatcher would somehow obligate me to purchase it. But the old woman was persistent. Her large eyes were filled with an intensity I had never seen in the eyes of the native people I had met during our visit. I looked at the dreamcatcher. It was beautiful. It had been handcrafted from crude materials, but with careful attention to each small detail. The feathers, which hung from the hoop, were perfectly matched and tied together with cords that appeared to be handmade.

I was certain the price of this exquisite creation would greatly exceed what I had intended to pay.

"It is very beautiful, but I only wanted a small one...for my office."

The young woman tried to explain to the old woman that I only wanted a small one. But the old woman shook her head and again thrust it toward me.

"How much?" I asked as I prepared to make an embarrassed exit.

The young woman again spoke briefly to the old woman. The old woman listened then shook her head furiously. The young woman shrugged.

"She said it was not for sale. It is a gift...for you!"

"But she must have spent <u>days</u> making it."

The young woman gestured as it if the whole matter was out of her hands. Again the old woman thrust the dreamcatcher toward me. This time she forcibly pushed it against my chest. When I at last closed my fingers around it, she turned and disappeared into the old trailer.

"I can't accept this as a gift..."

"She insists she made it for you, and she will not accept any money.

"But..."

"Please, sir. She wants you to have it." Again she shrugged to indicate she could do nothing further in the matter.

I looked at the baby who seemed to smile sympathetically at me. The big eyes revealed a degree of understanding and wisdom that would seem misplaced on one so young.

"I don't suppose she would begrudge me an opportunity to contribute to your child's education, would she?"

The young woman looked at me and then at the child. She smiled and gave me that 'what-can-I-do-about-it' shrug. I took all the paper money from my wallet and handed it to her.

"For the little one."

She reluctantly took the money. "For the little one", she agreed, with a broad smile. As we started to leave she said, "Graceful Raven...the name of the child...Graceful Raven." I nodded and waved good-bye to the woman and her little girl.

I still think about the three of them every single day...when I look at my beautiful dreamcatcher. I wonder about them as I see my dreams...one by one...becoming realities.

The Eighth Day

*I*n the beginning God created the heavens and the earth. The earth was without form and void, and darkness was upon the face of the deep; and the spirit of God was moving over the face of the waters.

And God said, "Let there be light"; and there was light. And God saw that the light was good; and God separated the light from the darkness. He called the light Day, and the darkness He called Night. And there was evening and there was morning, one day.

And God said, "Let there be a firmament in the midst of the waters, and let it separate the waters from the waters." And God made the firmament and separated the waters which were under the firmament from the waters which were above the firmament. And it was so. And God called the firmament Heaven. And there was evening and there was morning, a second day.

And God said, "Let the waters under the heavens be gathered together into one place, and let the dry land appear." And it was so.

God called the dry land Earth, and the waters that were gathered together He called Seas. And God saw it was good. And God said, "Let the Earth put forth vegetation, plants yielding seed, and fruit trees bearing fruit in which is their seed, each according to its kind, upon the Earth". And it was so. And God saw that it was good. And there was evening and there was morning, a third day.

And God said, "Let their be light in the firmament of the heavens to separate the day from the night; and let them be signs and for seasons and for days and years, and let them be lights in the firmament of the heavens to give light upon the earth." And it was so. And God made two great lights, the greater light to rule the day, and the lesser light to rule the night; He made the stars also. And God set them in the firmament of the heavens to give light upon the earth, to rule over the day and over the night, and to separate light from darkness. And God saw that it was good. And there was evening and there was morning, a fourth day.

And God said, "Let the waters bring forth swarms of living creatures, and let birds fly above the earth across the firmament of the heavens." So God created great sea monsters and every living creature that moves, with which the waters swarm, according to their kinds, and every winged creature according to its kind. And God saw that it was good. And God blessed them, saying, "Be fruitful and multiply and fill the waters in the seas, and let the birds multiply upon the earth." And there was evening and there was morning, a fifth day.

And God said, "Let the earth bring forth living creatures according to their kinds: cattle and creeping things and beasts of the earth according to their kinds." And it was so. And God saw that it was good.

Then God said, "Let us make man in our image, after our likeness; and let them have dominion over the fish of the sea, and over the birds of the air, and over cattle, and over all the earth, and over every creeping thing that creeps upon the earth." So God created man in his own image, in the image of God he created him; male and female he created them. And God blessed them, and God said to them, "Be fruitful and multiply, and fill the earth and subdue it; and have dominion over the fish of the sea and over the birds of the air and over every living thing that moves upon the earth." And God said, "Behold, I have given you every plant yielding seed which is upon the face of all the earth, and every tree with seed in its fruit; you shall have them for food. And to every beast of the earth, and to every bird of the air, and to everything that creeps on the earth, everything that has the breath of life, I have given every green plant for food."" And it was so. And God saw everything he had made, and behold, it was good. And there was evening and there was morning, a sixth day.

On the seventh day he rested....

Based upon the Book of Genesis, Chapters 1 and 2.

Following His day of rest, The Creator rose and surveyed the world He had created the previous week. He was especially pleased with the potential of mankind. He saw them as His children. He felt they could accomplish wondrous things in the years to come. But, as He looked ahead, He realized something more was needed. Mankind would need help from time to time. The people would need encouragement and support from other like-thinking human beings.

After some deliberation The Creator devised a plan. He would create a special breed of men and women that could help relieve some of this burden and allow Him more time to devote to other tasks...to the creating of other worlds.

He gave to each of these people special ears that would help them to hear and comprehend the true needs of each person they met.

To each He gave special eyes that could objectively and dispassionately view all facets of any problem...special eyes, that could discern both the complexities and the simplicities hidden within each issue.

To each He gave lips that were honest...that could speak only words of sincerity, compassion and truth.

And lastly He gave to each of these people a spirit-driven heart. This was most important because the spirit-driven heart would respond to His urgings. It was a heart that each individual could fill with truth and wisdom that He would provide as they encountered people in need of help and guidance. The Creator knew that the heart controlled the eyes, the ears, and the lips. A good heart...a heart filled with compassion and sincerity...would provide the proper guidance for these special organs.

When He had finished, The Creator summoned these special people together. He explained the importance of their work...that they were His representatives upon the Earth. He further explained that to deliberately mislead another person, or to provide any counsel short of their very best effort would be viewed by Him with great displeasure. Offenses would be punished by the loss of these special abilities.

With this final admonition He dispersed them across the width and breadth of the world. Some were sent to the mountains... some to the shores...some to the fields...and some to the cities. Still others would travel the lonely byways where mankind might wander in desperation.

As He sent them forth He touched each of them gently on their forehead and gave them a special name. He called them "true friends"!

And so as you continue your earth walk you are certain to meet some of these special people. They will be placed along your pathway in times of need to help you continue your progress. Helen Keller once said:

"Walking with a friend in the dark is better than walking alone in the light."

A friend is the most valuable of assets. The value of a true friend is incalculable...a friend is worth more than all the gold and silver in the world.

Thomas Fuller wrote:

"If you have one true friend, you have more than your share."

This is the absolute truth. If you have one 'true friend' you are truly blessed. However, in the course of your earth walk you will meet many who will willingly aid in your progress. It was a wise person who wrote:

"When it hurts to look back, and you're scared to look ahead, you can look beside you and your best friend will be there."

This was the special gift the Creator gave to each of us…on the Eighth day.

You're...

my friend

my companion,

through good times and bad

my friend, my buddy,

through happy and sad,

beside me you stand,

beside me you walk,

you're there to listen,

you're there to talk,

with happiness, with smiles,

with pain and tears,

I know you'll be there, throughout the years!

Author unknown

The Miracle of the Three Cacti

A few weeks ago my wife and I were hiking in Sedona. As is our custom we follow a trail to its end and meditate for awhile before heading back. These periods of reflection can work wonders for a writer. On this particular morning we were hiking the Little Horse Trail. It ends at a large bare rock with a spectacular view of a wide valley with mountains to the right and left.

As I sat there, completely absorbed in the silence, my eyes were drawn to a sheer cliff to my right. About two-thirds of the way down that wall of rock, on a space hardly bigger than a large boot print, were three cactus plants. By some freak of nature three seeds had landed on that spot and had clung there long enough to anchor themselves with a root system. This alone was no small feat, considering the heat of the Arizona sun and the winds that blow with an unforgiving frequency in that canyon. But somehow those tiny seeds held on and grew into mature plants. Somehow they endured the forces of nature. They shared the precious drops of water that fell during infrequent rains. By sharing…by cooperating, they survived.

So what can we learn from these three hardy survivors? First, it is safe to assume that of all the cactus seeds blowing through that particular canyon, at that particular point in time, those three were somehow destined to land together on that tiny ledge. They were destined to find the few inches of soil that would be hospitable enough to give them life.

Secondly, they only survived because they were content to share the available nourishment. Had one plant taken more than its share there is a good chance the others may not have survived. I can only speculate that a spirit of love kept these three seeds together long enough for them to grow into healthy, mature plants.

Thirdly, they had to cooperate. Just sharing is not enough. Cooperation was also critical. Only by working together could they survive.

But then I thought, suppose the seeds didn't all arrive at the same time...suppose one seed arrived first. That seed had a choice of all the available space, and all of the resources...the sunlight and water. The seed took root and began to grow. Then along came a second seed. The first had to learn to share the space and the resources with the newcomer. Somehow they were able to accomplish this, and the second seed began to grow. But then a third seed landed on that tiny piece of soil. The two cactus plants had to share what now had become tight quarters and sparse resources. But somehow the third plant also grew to maturity.

You see, these cactus plants learned a lesson we all need to learn. We all have <u>equal access</u>. This world we live in is not ours. We do not have an exclusive right to any of it. We did not create it. It was given to us...to all of us, to share.

We don't own the resources either. The warming sunlight...the refreshing and nourishing rains, are not the exclusive property of any one of us. They are given to us to share. Each of us is entitled to our fair share...just what we need to survive. It is only through cooperation and sharing that can we survive as a community...as a nation. The concepts of equal access, cooperation, and sharing form the core beliefs of every credo, every religion in the world. They are not alien concepts...they are the lessons we have been taught from childhood.

These plants will grow to maturity and eventually colorful blooms will appear on their appendages. Shortly after the blooms appear most cactus plants will begin to die. And so it is with each of us. We are born. We learn the important lessons of life...we seek out our destiny, we learn the art of sharing, we learn to cooperate, we bloom...and then we pass on. Like the cactus plants we have fulfilled our Purpose. We have lived our allotted time. We have fulfilled our destiny. Hopefully, for a brief period of time we have made the world a better place by our presence.

As you go through life take a lesson from those three plants living high on that wall of solid rock. Actively seek out your destiny...your life's Purpose. Find contentment in whatever state you find yourself. Always seek to grow and to improve your lot. But do it with a contented heart. Learn to share. Even when you have only enough for yourself…especially when you only have enough for yourself. When you can do this you will have mastered the secret of lasting abundance.

Motivation vs. Inspiration

Following a recent workshop, a young woman asked me an interesting question. She wanted to know if I considered myself a motivational speaker, or an inspirational speaker. Since that day I have given that question some thought and, after discussing the subject with several friends in the speaking and training profession, have concluded that while it is generally perceived that a motivational program can get people fired up, the over all effect tends to be short-term. However an inspirational speech can have a deeper impact on a person, possibly even causing a life-long change.

This is a point often overlooked by leaders. It is relatively simple to motivate an employee in the short run...a contest, a performance bonus, an additional perquisite, even a pep talk may achieve the desired results. There is certainly nothing wrong with trying to improve performance using these incentives. But, if these programs are misused and people begin to feel manipulated, the positive impact is soon diluted. Studies have shown that employees often resent motivational programs when they feel the employer is just trying to get more work out of them.

An effective leader should attempt to inspire people...to bring about the conditions that will cause positive long-term changes. Today too many people see their jobs as boring and unfulfilling. Employee loyalty and involvement is not as prevalent as it once was. Even jobs that might appear exciting and desirable to some people may be unsatisfactory to those who have them. Logan Piersall Smith once wrote that "the test of a true calling is the love of the drudgery it requires". With a little effort an effective leader can help make almost any job seem more gratifying.

A meaningful vision, combined with a strong sense of purpose can be instrumental in helping a person recognize the value of their effort. Objectives that help an individual stretch and grow, as a person can be beneficial. Developed properly they can inspire over a long period of time.

Some leaders may be quick to say, "But I'm not a motivator... I'm not the outgoing, gregarious type. I can't jump up and down and get people excited!"

You don't have to! Besides, that behavior tends to wear thin after a while.

Here are a few tips that can help you "inspire" your people over the long-term:

- Build credibility and trust. Let your people see that your word stands for something. People like working for a leader they can believe in. An organization built on a sense of mutual trust can usually sustain itself, even during difficult times.

- Help the people understand the importance and value of their work. People become enthusiastic when they realize that they can make a difference.
- Provide opportunities for people to master new tasks and to expand their skills. People grow when they are called upon to continually overcome new challenges. Ronald Osborn said, "Unless you try to do something beyond that which you have already mastered, you will never grow."
- Help people learn good judgment. The most recent issue of the Boy Scout Manual points out that "good judgment can't be taught, but through the gathering of many experiences, it can be learned." An inspirational leader is one who takes the time necessary to help his/her people learn the skills needed to exercise good judgment. These skills include the ability to recognize all available options, to select the best solution, and finally to effectively implement the decision.

The Bellringer

A stranger approached a well-dressed man on the street the other day.

"Hey, there. Excuse me...do you have a minute?"

The well-dressed man turned. "Yes?"

"A funny thing just happened...I would like to tell you about it."

The man looked startled and began to move away.

"No, no. Don't go...please," said the stranger as he took hold of his arm. "This is important"

The man hesitated. He looked around as if he was about to summon help to deal with this intrusion on his mid-day walk.

"I must tell you about The Bellringer!"

"The what?"

"Let me begin at the beginning. I was walking down the street a short while ago, when I came upon a man ringing a bell. I thought perhaps he was deranged, or something. He was wearing rather strange clothing, and he had a sad, faraway look on his face. He looked tired...

exhausted. But he had the look of a man with a mission. I asked what he was doing. He said he was trying to wake the people.

"But, sir", I said. "It is the middle of the day. People have been up and about for hours."

"Oh, no," said he. " I'm trying to <u>really</u> waken them!"

"I'm afraid I don't understand."

"Every so often...every generation, or so, I have to travel around and ring my bell to get people's attention. They seem to get into a rut. They lose the ability to see things clearly...to reason. My job is to rouse them...to get their attention...to get them to think about what's going on around them. Sometimes to alert them to a danger."

"Are you usually successful?"

"Oh my, yes." Then he paused. "Well, sometimes...actually, not often enough. But I can't stop trying."

"What is the danger you are so concerned about?"

"I'm concerned about the alarming rate at which you people are wasting the resources that took so many years to build. You live for today...with little or no thought for the future. You would take the last few pennies from those who work to build your resource base, and yet throw millions of dollars at people who contribute only marginally, if at all."

"I must have looked puzzled, so he continued."

"You pay people who are slightly more physically gifted, excessive amounts to compete in games. You pay entertainers to insult you and present programs that lower your standards and corrupt your youth. You pay corporate leaders enormous sums to destroy capital they had no part in creating...for what amounts to short-term gratification." He paused as if to add further emphasis. "If this isn't waste, I don't know what is!"

"Wait a minute," I said. "I understand about athletes and performers who are overpaid. But corporate leaders do contribute to the resource base."

"Some do...some do not!"

"Explain, please".

"Awhile back...a few generations ago...there were men among you who built great industrial empires. They created wealth in steel, oil, and chemicals. They built the automobile industry. They built the railroad system that moved people and goods back and forth across the country, making the accumulation of wealth possible for many, many people. But these people were often ridiculed. Newspapers criticized them. Cartoons depicted them as 'robber barons'. And yet they created jobs that have lasted for generations."

"But they exploited people...they paid low wages."

The Bellringer laughed. "Wages that were so low they brought people from all over the world to your shores...people who proclaimed this "the land of opportunity". With these wages people built homes...educated their children. Many of these people made fortunes from the opportunities created by the so-called 'robber barons'. In short they created this tremendous resource base that has been multiplied many times over as the years passed."

"So?"

"So now you have taken it for granted. You believe this source of wealth will last forever. And yet, as we speak, other men and women are rapidly dismantling these resources. They do it in the name of 'efficiency'. They claim it is a new way of building wealth. They claim their methods are so sophisticated that only they can understand them. After all, they say, 'Wall Street is happy...and the stockholders are delighted! What could possibly be wrong?'" He paused for a moment to see if I grasped his point. "In the name of short-term returns they are destroying capital that took years to accumulate. They are not building resources, they are not making them more efficient, and they are <u>destroying</u> them. And they are being heavily compensated for doing it! That's why I ring my bell in the middle of the day! That's why I try to wake people up! People <u>should</u> be compensated, and compensated <u>well</u>, for enhancing the resources...for building companies and creating jobs. They should <u>not</u> be compensated for destroying wealth in the name of short-term returns. Resources, wealth, and jobs are not to be taken for granted. If a job fails to add value to the resource base it should be changed so that it does add value. Those who can add value should receive the higher compensation. What took generations to build must not be destroyed. It must be used as a basis upon which the future can be built." The Bellringer looked very tired, but he smiled. "I thank you for your time, my friend. Any help you can give me will be greatly appreciated."

"And with that he turned and continued down the street. I watched him until he disappeared around the corner...and that's when I saw you. I wanted you to hear his story."

The well-dressed man shook his hand and walked away deep in thought.

"Excuse me, ma'am. Do you have a minute? There is something I would like to share with you. You see, there was this Bellringer..."

Ginger

I honestly know how or why it happened. I have no excuses…it just happened. I was vacationing in Canada when I met Ginger. For reasons I can not explain I was immediately attracted to her. She was a real beauty, with long blond hair and large, sad-looking brown eyes. When I first saw her she gave me what I took as a come hither look. I admit I was surprised and maybe a bit shocked. Our age difference was apparent. She was only eighteen…and I was past the mid-point of life.

We had barely been introduced when she walked over and brushed up against me. I was intimidated. I consider myself somewhat of a man of the world. I am educated. I have traveled extensively. And yet I have never met anyone like Ginger. As hard as I tried to resist she continued her advancements. I knew it was futile to resist her.

In my entire lifetime I have never paid for the services of a female. But then again I had never met anyone quite like Ginger. Somehow I knew that she would be worth the price, no matter what it might be. So I succumbed to my desires and completed the financial arrangements necessary to possess her, even though it would be for such a short time.

And as I had anticipated, our time together was well worth the price. In spite of her comparative youth Ginger proved to quite knowledgeable in matters of her trade. She showed me things I had only dreamed about. She provided me with a variety of physical experiences like nothing I had ever had in the past. When we had finished our time together I was completely spent. I was breathing heavily…my knees were weak. But Ginger was fresh as a daisy. Even though I had given her my best, she was ready to move on to someone else. I was saddened to think that the experience that had meant so much to me had meant so little to her.

Still I can't stop thinking about her. Those big eyes…that tousled mop of blond hair…her strong body will probably always remain deep in my memory. I guess that is the way it is supposed to be when someone has been a part of such a memorable experience in one's life.

If you are ever in Jasper Park in Alberta, Canada I hope you will stop by to say 'Hello' to Ginger. She is a very special horse…she gave my very first riding lesson.

The Tenth Wave

Ever since I was a small boy I have been enthralled by stories of the sea. Once a distant relative of mine paid a visit to my grandparents. He spent the better part of a Sunday afternoon telling us tales of his years as the captain of a fair-sized fishing boat. I was particularly interested in a story about 'the ninth wave'. According to the old skipper the ninth wave is the one furthest away…the one on the horizon. In his experience that was where the fishing was the best. He said that if you could steer your boat along the ninth wave you would always have a good catch. He swore on his mother's soul that this was the 'gospel truth'.

Over the years I've heard any number of stories about the ninth wave. Some said it was a good omen, others swore with equal verve that it was evil and deadly. I also heard that the ninth wave was a rare phenomenon caused by an unusual blend of weather conditions.

The last time I was at the shore I decided to check it out for myself. I found a comfortable perch on an old pier where I would not disturb the dozen or so fishermen who had settled in for the day. I began to count the waves as they rolled over the shore below me. By my observations the ninth wave was identical to the first. I counted another nine waves...same result. They all looked alike. And from the activity of the fishermen I would guess the ninth produced no more fish than the other eight. I counted another nine waves. Again the same result. They were all the same. Same size...same speed... same gentle roll across the beach. As I counted still another nine waves I began to notice something strange. They were *not* all the same. Each had a slightly different speed...each hit the shore at a slightly different angle. Some broke to the left, and some broke to the right. Some hit directly on the shoreline. There were differences in the height of each wave...in the way it broke over the beach...and the distance it traveled across the sand...even in the length of the swell between each individual wave.

To the casual observer one would seem pretty much like all the others...a constant parade of sameness, rolling from some far away land to this shore. But from my observations I could see many differences. In fact, the longer I watched the more distinct each wave became. In like manner each day, to some people, might seem pretty much like any other day. They each bring their routine. We get up at the same time each day. We work the same number of hours. We tend to eat our meals at about the same time. Everything is pretty much the same.

And yet I assure you that each day is different. Each day has particular nuances that make it unique. Life's pleasure comes from being able to recognize these subtle differences and taking full advantage of them. This is important because if you can't recognize and appreciate the nuances of each passing day you will never be able to recognize and appreciate the <u>tenth</u> day…the day that lies just beyond the horizon.

Living a Committed Life

Lately I have been thinking a great deal about a growing problem in our society. We as a people are suffering from lack of 'commitment' in all aspects of life. Nowadays people seem less likely to have commitment to their jobs. Not too many years ago a person took a job with the expectation of remaining there for the bulk of their career. They made a commitment to their company. It may not have been a written commitment, but it was a form of commitment, nonetheless. You took a job…you learned your trade…you became more proficient…you earned more money…you provided for your family…and eventually you retired. Of course, in all fairness, organizations seemed to be more committed to their employees in those days than they have evidenced of late. Our business leaders…and our politicians…should consider the words of Vince Lombardi:

> "Individual commitment to a group effort—that is what makes a team work, a company work, a society work, a civilization work."

We also seem to be less committed to each other. More people choose to start families without a formal commitment. They have children when they aren't yet ready to make a commitment to each other. I don't mean to sound judgmental, but doesn't that seem a bit absurd...to be bringing new souls into the world when you are not yet ready to have a committed relationship? As Alfred Adler once wrote:

"We only regard those unions as real examples of love and real marriages in which a fixed and unalterable decision has been taken. If men and women contemplate an escape, they do not collect all their powers for the task. In none of the serious and important tasks of life do we arrange such a "getaway." We cannot love and be limited."

Confucius said much the same thing:

"Wheresoever you go, go with all your heart."

And from the number of empty parking spaces you can see at many of our churches and synagogues each weekend, it would appear that our commitment to a spiritual life is also on the decrease. This is especially distressing when you consider the serious social issues that face all of us today. When creating the Constitution Thomas

Jefferson may have anticipated the need for greater commitment when he wrote:

"We mutually pledge to each other our lives, our fortunes, and our sacred honor."

A life without commitment is not a complete life...something always seems to be lacking. When you are committed to what I like to refer to as the 'life forces' life seems to take on more meaning. A person becomes happier...more at peace with themselves and the world around them.

As I see it the primary 'life forces' are your job, your family, and your spiritual life. Throughout this book you will find a number of references to these issues and how they combine to make ones life more meaningful.

It is my belief that nothing really happens until a commitment has been established. I guess W. H Murray sums up my thinking best with this quote from "<u>The Scottish Himalayan Expedition</u>":

"Until one is committed, there is hesitancy...the moment one commits oneself, then Providence moves, too. All sorts of things occur to help one that would never otherwise occurred."

Commitment becomes the catalyst for the blessings that lead to a more abundant life. So how can you benefit from increasing the level of commitment in these important aspects of your life? First, let's talk about your job. Many people complain that their jobs are dull, routine, and boring. Some see their job as menial work. They find it difficult to commit to a job they dislike so much. E. M. Gray wrote:

> **"The successful person has the habit of doing the things failures don't like to do. They don't like doing them either necessarily. But their disliking is subordinated to the strength of their purpose."**

Noted writer and inspirational speaker, Wayne Dyer, says:

> **"There's no scarcity of opportunity to make a living at what you love. There is only a scarcity of resolve to make it happen."**

In other words, the missing link to loving the job is 'commitment'. Quite frankly people who dislike their work have a decision to make. They can always leave and find a job they like better. Milton Garland offers an even better suggestion. He Wrote:

> **"My advice is to go into something and stay with it until you like it. You can't like it until you**

obtain expertise in that work. And once you are an expert, it's a pleasure."

This is good advice. It is another way of describing commitment. You might also think about the job in terms of the benefits it presents to others. How do others benefit from the effort you put forth? What you may see as menial and meaningless tasks may be viewed by the Universe as very important. Most jobs include some tasks that are less interesting than others. Some may even seem like drudgery. But by being able to look beyond those tasks you may see the true beauty and value in the work you do. Someone once wrote:

"The nature of a true calling is a love for the drudgery it involves."

As to making a commitment to your family you should think about what constitutes a 'family'. Ideally a family is made up of two people who love each other, and who are committed to making their relationship grow and flourish. At some point they may decide they are ready to accept the added responsibility of children, and the family begins to expand. Think about what this means. Children are really sweet souls on loan to us by a loving and caring Creator. They are ours for a short time to care for, to nurture, to guide…to love. When you think in these terms it is relatively simple to make a proper commitment to the concept of 'family'.

However, making a commitment to your family is not a simple matter. There are times when you will be confronted with difficulty...times of adversity...times when you will question your ability to stay the course. But I can assure you the commitment you make to your family...the hours you invest in your spouse and children...will play enormous dividends in the years to come. It will become the most rewarding commitment you will ever make. Vince Lombardi wrote:

"The quality of a person's life is in direct proportion to their commitment to excellence".

In matters related to issues of job and family I must say that 'compromise' and 'commitment' often go hand in hand. It is often difficult to sustain a commitment to these two issues without some compromise. You will find that the word 'commitment' most often refers to your long-term relationship with the issue...while in the short term some compromise may be necessary.

There will be times when your 'commitment' might conflict in some way with the 'commitment' of a coworker or family member. You should be prepared to offer a compromise to enable all parties to achieve their commitments. This in no way means you should lessen your degree of commitment...it only means you should recognize and abet another person when their commitment conflicts with yours. It won't happen often, but you should always be cognizant of the commitments of others.

I find it a bit more difficult to wrap the issue of spiritual life into a nice, neat definition. Spirituality means different things to different people. One definition I am fond of using is the one that goes something like this...

> **"Religion is for the people who fear Hell...spirituality is for those who have <u>been</u> there."**

This definition has a special significance to many of the people I have worked with who are overcoming problems with addiction. To most of these folks overcoming their addictions are like climbing out of Hell. I have been especially blessed in that I have never had a problem with addiction, but I can relate to their perspective. I can certainly understand how spirituality can help them through their struggles.

In discussing commitment as it relates to matters of the spirit, John Wesley wrote:

> **"Do all the good you can,**
> **By all the means you can,**
> **In all the ways you can,**
> **In all the places you can,**
> **At all the times you can,**

To all the people you can,
As long as ever you can."

When I am sitting here on the mountaintop looking at the beauty that surrounds me…or looking the broad expanse of an ocean…or walking in the solitude of the desert, I have no problem understanding the true nature of spirituality. At those special times I can readily understand what spirituality is and how it impacts my personal belief system.

But how can I put that into words that will be meaningful to you, the reader? A spiritual life is not as tangible…it is not as easy to put your arms around as a job, or a family. But it is just as important an issue when you are attempting to live a balanced life.

The beauty of commitment often lies in the fact that you don't have to reach a state of perfection to make a commitment and to receive the benefits from it. Even when you commit your 'imperfect self' to a <u>positive</u> course of action the Universe will ultimately guide you to your life's Purpose.

You see, when you make a commitment to these issues, you are not expected to be perfect. You are still a human being, subject to human frailties. As Marian Wright Edelman wrote:

"You are not obligated to win. You're obligated to keep trying to do the best you can every day."

Perhaps Albert Einstein best sums up the essence of commitment as it applies to a person's life when he writes:

> **"Try not to become a man of success, but rather to become a man of value. He is considered successful in our day who gets more out of life than he puts in. But a man of value will give more than he receives."**

Mark Twain also wrote something related to commitment that I feel is also good advice:

> **"Twenty years from now you will be more disappointed by the things that you didn't do than by the ones you did do. So throw off the bowlines. Sail away from the safe harbor. Catch the trade winds in your sails. Explore. Dream. Discover."**

So I say to you, go forth in confidence. Make your commitments. Live the abundant life.

Stained Glass Windows

When I lived in the city one of my favorite pastimes was to visit the cathedral. I would sit for a time…sometimes for hours…in an empty pew and meditate. Being alone with my thoughts has always been a source of pleasure to me, especially as I have grown older. It gives me an opportunity to reflect on my life's experiences…something I rarely took the time to do as those experiences were unfolding. I've since learned that a greater pleasure comes from savoring these moments when they are occurring…to enjoy them as one is living them. But as I sped through my life I did not spend a great deal of time reflecting on these precious moments…and the people who shared them with me.

In time I realized that a great part of my enjoyment of those periods of meditation was enhanced by the colors that filled the vastness of the cathedral as the sunlight poured through the stained glass windows. Alone in the solitude of the great cathedral I could understand what she meant when psychiatrist Elizabeth Keble-Ross wrote:

"People are like stained-glass windows. They sparkle and shine when the sun is out, but when the darkness sets in their true beauty is revealed only if there is a light from within."

It's funny how the presence of color seems to add to the reflective experience. Now I find that my enjoyment of those reflective moments amid the color and solitude of the cathedral has followed me to my mountain. I realize as I sit alone on my mountain it is much like the cathedrals in the city. The vastness and the bright colors…they are all right here. Especially when I come here early in the morning. The first rays of the dawn waken the colors of the rocks and unveil a dazzling splash of color. I can't help but think of John Muir's observation:

"How glorious a greeting the sun gives the mountains."

Throughout the day the colors seem to change as the shadows move back and forth across the various rock formations. It creates a spiritual ambiance…just like the cathedrals. Aldous Huxley must certainly have understood this when he wrote:

"My father considered a walk among the mountains as the equivalent of churchgoing."

The mountain vistas become special places where thoughts come freely and remembrances can be plucked from the past and savored over and over again. Ideas flow as freely as the nearby stream. It is like Raymond Inmon described when he wrote:

**"If you are seeking creative ideas, go out walking.
Angels speak to a man when he goes for a walk."**

At these times I am certain the Creator is present, for He must take a great deal of pleasure looking at Nature's equivalent of the man-made stained-glass windows in the city's cathedrals. They must mean just as much to Him as it does to all of us.

Fences

As I look out over the vastness that extends in every direction I am aware that there are no boundaries. It is as if the Creator wanted to make this beautiful paradise free from any limitations. It gives the impression that all this vastness…this great beauty…is free for the taking. That any person—man, woman, or child—has open access to it all. The majestic mountains, the lush valleys, the endless streams…the changing colors and shadows as the day matures, are here for everyone to enjoy…without any restrictions.

It is so unlike the city, where fences set limitations on every aspect of life. Fences are important, I guess, to many people. Certainly there are times when fences are necessary. There are times when they may be necessary to enclose and protect the people we hold dear to us, while keeping the undesirable elements out. Robert Frost once wrote:

> **"Don't take down a fence unless you are sure why it was put up."**

Someone once said:

"The fence that makes good neighbors needs a gate to make good friends."

Fences prevent us from knowing what lies on the other side. They can keep us from learning about other people…their different beliefs…their needs. Is what we keep locked up by our fences so valuable and irreplaceable that it warrants such protection…at the cost of the knowledge we could gain if it wasn't there? Is what it encloses so valuable that we can't share it with those on the other side? Could the removal of all fences build a better understanding of our neighbors? Could it promote a better sense of good will? Does a fence serve any useful purpose? Does a fence only contribute to misunderstanding and distrust?

As for me, I prefer to be where nothing blocks the beauty of my world. I know I can't keep it for myself…nor would I want to…it is really not mine. It is here for everyone and everyone should have open access to it. But aside from that, do fences only keep us apart? Do they only promote and amplify any differences that might exist between us? Dan Miller wrote in his book, **48 Days to the Work You Love**:

"You know, we have our differences, every one does…honest, real differences. But I do believe

strongly that we as neighbors are drawn together far more than we are driven apart."

I guess the main mystique about fences is that we all tend to believe that the grass is always greener on the other side. But Robert Fulghum makes a good point when he says:

"The grass is not always greener on the other side of the fence. Fences have nothing to do with it. The grass is greenest where it is watered. When crossing over fences, carry water with you and tend the grass wherever you may be."

I don't have all the answers. I only know that in my world...on my mountaintop, I have no need for fences. What I have here is yours. You are welcome to all I have to share...particularly my thoughts and dreams. Consider these words of Robert Green Ingersoll:

"Surely there is grandeur in knowing that in the realm of thought, at least, you are without a chain; that you have the right to explore all heights and depth; that there are no walls nor fences, nor prohibited places, nor sacred corners in all the vast expanse of thought."

I guess Ralph Waldo Emerson should have the final word...he wrote:

> **"As long as civilization is essentially one of property, of fences, of exclusiveness, it will be mocked by delusions. Our riches will leave us sick, there will be bitterness in our laughter, and our wine will burn in our mouth. Only that good profits, which we can all taste with all doors open, and which serves all men."**

Looking up...when you can't look down

As I write this I am sitting next to a medicine wheel at a vortex in Sedona, Arizona. Looking up from this spot I can see a blue sky crisscrossed by vapor trails from airplanes headed who knows where. In all directions I can see mountainous rock formations. To my left they are primarily red; to my right, and directly in front of me, they are white. A creamy beige, to be more precise. These mountains speak to me of strength and a sense of eternal foreverness... they will be exactly the same every time I return to this spot.

I think back to my childhood when I had a great fear of heights. I had regular nightmares in which I dreamed of falling from the Empire State Building. This was strange dream for a boy born and raised in Wellsville, Ohio...where the tallest building is five stories high. Years later when I was in New York City I happened to be walking past the dreaded skyscraper. I walked back and forth a number of times before I had the courage to go up to the observation deck. When I got there I slowly walked to the edge and timidly looked over. As I placed my hands on the top of the wall I swear I felt it move. I let out a yelp and jumped back. Everyone on the deck at the time looked at me in amusement. I again inched my way to the wall and looked over the edge. The cars and people below looked like ants. I looked over several times. Each time I ventured to the edge the view seemed less and less frightening.

Later, when I lived in the city, I made several trips to the top of the building. By then I could look over without any fear of falling. In fact, when I did stand-up comedy I used to joke that I no longer feared 'heights', but now I was afraid of 'widths'.

When I lived in Washington, D.C. I heard a sermon delivered by my friend Reverend Roger Gench, the pastor at the New York Avenue Presbyterian Church. Reverend Gench talked about a hike he and his wife Frances took at Chasm Lake in Rocky Mountain National Park. He said there was a particular trail that involved negotiating a narrow ledge along a steep cliff. At one point there was a 200-foot stretch where path was only four feet wide, but to a person with a fear of falling the trail seemed even narrower. Somehow he managed to complete the hike, even though he admits his knees were weak and his stomach was in knots.

To his surprise, when they took the hike again this year, he was able to walk to the edge of the ledge and look down. Later he was discussing the experience with an experienced mountain climber. The veteran climber said this was not surprising. He said people with a fear of heights often overcome the fear by exposing themselves to the fear time and time again.

As I think back over my experiences, and those of Reverend Gench, I realize the truth about fear. Every one of us has fears. We fear the dark. We fear failure and poverty. We fear being alone. We fear the loss of a loved one. We fear growing old. We fear sickness... and death. We all fear something. Often there are times in our lives when the fear seems absolutely paralyzing. But the more we confront our fears...the more we address them face-to-face the less they seem so terrifying.

But even as we are confronting our fears it is important to realize that we have a constant support system. Even when these fears seem completely overwhelming, our Creator is always by our side. The Creator is like these mountains in front of me... solid, omnipresent, and constantly there, wherever I turn. And it will always be that way. He was present when these rock formations were created and He will be there long after they have been reduced to insignificant dust.

His strength is far greater, even than these towering monuments to peace and beauty. Here I can stand at the edge of a sharp precipice and instead of feeling fragile and afraid, I feel that I am part of all this. I am no longer fearful. I return to the medicine wheel and touch the rock that forms the exact center. As I touch that rock I pray that I might find words that give each of you a sense of strength in the knowledge that you will never be given a burden too heavy for you to lift...or a fear you cannot overcome by looking upwards. Look up to find the strength to face your greatest fears.

A peace perspective… from an old dove

Some days when I lack the inspiration to write I just sit and read. On this particular day I was reading the newspaper. As I recall I was reading several articles about the various armed conflicts that were in the news at the time. I was turning the page when I heard a rustling noise just above my head. I turned and was shocked to see a dove perched on a low hanging tree limb. The dove seemed disturbed.

"Excuse me, I know it is rude to read over a person's shoulder, but I wanted to finish that article."

"I beg your pardon?'

"You just turned the page and I have been trying to finish reading that article."

"What article?"

"That one about the war. I had started reading it this morning at the coffee shop, but some pigeons had been reading it earlier and you know how messy they can be."

I must have looked surprised so he went on.

"Someone had left a paper at the coffee shop and I was reading that article, but the pigeons had…well you know."

"Birds can read?" I stammered.

"Of course! We are quite literate. We read every chance we get."

I was still confused. I rubbed my eyes and looked at him again. I couldn't tell for certain which surprised me the most…that a dove could talk…or that he could read a newspaper.

"You actually read…you read newspapers?"

"Yes. Birds love to read. We read books…magazines… anything we can get our claws on. Being a dove, I try to read everything I can find related to conflict and peace efforts."

"Are you putting me on? A bird that is concerned about war and peace?"

He became indignant.

"Why not? Birds suffer and get killed because of your stupid wars just as much as humans do!"

"I never thought about that."

"Of course not. Like all humans you think birds are just here for your amusement. You like us only when we sing for you, or when we fill your bellies. Other than that you consider us to a nuisance."

"You're unfair!"

"Am I? When did you ever think about us birds?"

"I have always had a birdfeeder in my yard. I have a bush in my backyard that is always filled with hummingbirds. When I lived in Pennsylvania I had a pheasant walk through my yard every single day!"

"Are you telling me some of your best friends are birds?"

"I suppose that does sound silly… But I am interested in the fact that you read so much."

"Well, it is not easy. Birds usually have to read on the wing, so to speak. When we are flying overhead, or sitting in a tree, we are trying to read, if at all possible."

"I see."

"Of course it is not all that easy. I spend a lot of time hanging around universities where students sometimes leave books and magazines laying around. Actually books are easier for us to read than newspapers…it is easier to turn the pages."

"I suppose you are going to tell me you have read 'War and Peace'?"

"Are you kidding? That book weighs a ton! But I have read the Cliff Notes."

"Are you serious?"

"Of course."

"Well that puts you on a par with many college students."

"A great deal has been written about war and peace…and a lot of it makes sense to me."

"Such as…?"

"Well, Einstein said…

"A country cannot simultaneously prepare for and prevent war."

"You certainly have read a great deal about the subject. I would have to say that you must be the leading authority on the subject…at least in the bird kingdom."

"I don't know about that…a lot of us have an interest in the subject. On both sides, as a matter of fact. And that has created a bit of a problem."

"How so?"

"We doves don't have the greatest eyesight. Sometimes we have to depend on others to read for us. When that happens we are never quite sure when we are getting the straight story."

"I don't get it."

"Well, everyone knows hawks have great eyesight…so sometimes we have to depend on them to pass on to us the news of the day."

"That's nice…I mean it is sort of symbiotic when one species can be helpful to another."

"Well, the problem is…at least for us doves…we don't always get the straight story from the hawks. You see hawks don't see all the issues the same as we do. They are not a peaceful breed. They are warlike…they actually seem to prefer conflict and wars. So when they read news stories related to conflict they have a distinctly different perspective."

"I see. That could present a problem."

"Oh, it does. Every bit of news we get through them is filtered through their particular bias. Since they are so partial to conflict they can see justification for war that often doesn't exist. They see enemies behind every tree. They see weaponry that others do not see. To a hawk most other living creatures are potential enemies."

"So how do you and your friends know what is true and what is the result of this bias?"

"Sometimes it is very confusing. It causes conflict among the rest of us. We often squabble among ourselves. We end up taking sides and wasting time debating issues, which are not really relevant to our daily lives. It distracts our attention from the things we should be concerned over...like conservation and economic issues."

"Birds worry over conservation and economic issues?"

"Of course, if you don't have enough land and water to sustain your needs, how are we going to survive. We use the same land...we drink water the same as humans. When the country is at war, money is deflected for arms that could be used elsewhere...to benefit all of us. It is like General Dwight Eisenhower said..."

> **"Every gun that is made, every warship launched, every rocket fired signifies, in the final sense, a theft from those who hunger and are not fed, those who are cold and not clothed."**

"So peace issues are quite a concern to you and the other birds?"

"Some are less concerned than others. But in my case you can see the degree of concern I carry over these issues."

"What do you mean?"

"Doves are supposed to be white…you may have noticed my feathers have turned prematurely grey!"

"Point well taken. But suffering from wars is not a new issue. President John F. Kennedy may have summed it up best when he wrote…

> **"Man must put an end to war, or war will put a end to mankind."**

"Amen to that. President Lincoln once wrote…

> **"The best way to destroy an enemy is to make him a friend."**

"Well said, my friend. Well said.

Hopes and Dreams

Today I am sitting on the set of a new television show. No doubt before this is published the show will either succeed or fail— based on the viewing habits of a fickle public. I've have been hired for two days as an 'extra'. That means I will sit for several days waiting to be a part of several scenes in one of the upcoming episodes. The scenes themselves may or may not be critical to the success or failure of the series. They will have no role in my success or failure as an actor, because I will probably not be recognizable even to my family and friends.

However, I am struck by the faces of the other people who have come, just as I have, in pursuit of some degree of fame. As faces go, these are well above average. They are pretty, or handsome, as the case may. They are distinctive. Each possesses a certain look...a desire to be seen and to please.

Some of these faces will go on to achieve undreamed of success in "show business". Others will achieve success in completely different arenas. Some will never achieve the dreams and aspirations they pursue. Some will always feel they failed...and perhaps some will accept a lifestyle far below that which was intended as their destiny.

This is sad. I suspect the people behind these faces are well above average intelligence and ambition. They are capable of making major contributions. This group is a microcosm of society. There is confidence, sincerity, vulnerability, even arrogance and indifference. A few of us, older and perhaps a bit wiser because of our life experiences, have learned a great deal more about life and have adjusted our expectations.

The real difference is in the eyes. In the eyes the real truth is more evident. Through the eyes you can penetrate the facade and see the real person. Through the eyes you can see the reality. You can see the eagerness, the determination, and even the desperation.

How can I tell these young faces that what happens here today will not ultimately define them as a person. Success or failure, <u>today</u>, will not determine who they are. Nor will define the person they can become. What I would love to tell them is that whatever happens today will not define them as a person. Whether they achieve their dreams or not, they will not be limited in any way by today's events. Failure <u>today</u> does not create any barrier to the future that awaits you tomorrow. Confucius said it best:

> **"Our greatest glory is not in never falling, but in rising each time we fall."**

You see, we are all going to fail at something. That is a fundamental law of nature. We will not be successful at everything we attempt. That is impossible. One of the things that may be a small advantage to us older folks is that we have seen failure...we have felt rejection...we have experienced desperate times...and we have lived through them. We know that no matter how serious the 'failure', there are always some successes just beyond the horizon. At times you just have to tread water for a little while to get beyond the dark days.

Some people will always define themselves in terms of isolated events. That is sheer folly. Any failure you experience today is just one step on the ladder of success. Regardless of what happens today...a fresh new tomorrow is waiting.

A Good Cigar

The smoke swirls and dances skyward. A nearby waterfall tumbles down a steep cliff. Its soft roar adds to the serenity rather than detracting from it.

My cigar burns slowly as if to prolong the moment…a part of nature contributing to the appreciation of Nature. To some folks it may seem politically incorrect or insensitive to speak of smoking with such reverence…to speak of a cigar and the beauty of nature in the same breath. I plead for a moment of understanding and indulgence. As I sit here, I just can't see how Nature and a good cigar could possibly represent a conflict. I would like to think a good cigar tends to bring out the best in a person.

I think a good cigar makes me more reflective. I believe I am better able to see my life as it was…and is. I think back over all the stages of my life, from childhood to the present. I can see clearly my successes…and my failures. I see where I have done a good job…and where I could have done better. I think about my childhood…about growing up in a small town in southern Ohio. There were happy times and times that were not so joyous. I learned the fundamentals of life from a small town perspective. I learned about honesty and the value of hard work. I learned that nothing worthwhile comes without effort and sacrifice. Those were my formative years. I think about the happiness I received years later as I watched my children come into the world, grow up, and mature into the productive citizens they have become. I remember the people I befriended, and those I should have gotten to know better. I think about all the people I have been able to help during my journey... and the people I have harmed. It is easy to see all these things so clearly as I enjoy my cigar.

I think a good cigar makes me less judgmental. When I am enjoying my cigar I find it difficult to make judgments about other people. I think about the people who have wronged me over the years, but just briefly. In these moments it is difficult to be angry with other people. After all they are just people, subject to the same frailties and weaknesses I have exhibited from time to time. Probably they never meant me any real harm. With a few exceptions it probably wasn't even deliberate. And after all, how harmful was it...really? I survived. In fact I may have even benefited in some way from the experience. At any rate I find it hard to judge them harshly when I am enjoying my cigar.

At these times I find it difficult to think of other people solely in terms of our differences. We are all human beings. We are all trying to find our way along our earth walk. I don't believe that as I sit here

Musings from the Mountaintop

I would have a problem with anyone who sat down beside me. I think we would be able to look beyond our differences, and just enjoy the moment. Issues between us would fade away as we sat and talked. Maybe it could be that way with nations. If our leaders could just sit together and talk out their differences over a good cigar. Maybe they could find a way to end wars, and famine, and poverty. Maybe over a good cigar they could see that their differences are really rather insignificant in comparison to their similarities.

I think a good cigar makes a person more spiritual. Solitude and a good cigar cause a person to think more about the spiritual side of life. Maybe it is merely the beauty of my surroundings...the roar of the waterfall...the colorful mountains...or the graceful flight of the eagle overhead. A good cigar only adds to the moment. It all seems so clear now. At this moment I can truly understand the importance of living in the moment. And I do enjoy the moment. My cigar...the beauty of my surroundings, all make me want to experience the moment...to bask in it...to relish every second of it.

Invariably I gravitate to thoughts about what was intended to be...to what the Creator had in mind when He put this all together. He certainly had higher aspirations for His world. No doubt He envisioned a world of peace and prosperity for all its inhabitants. No doubt He wanted all of His people to be able to see and appreciate His masterpiece. Most will never have the opportunity to see it as I have seen it. I fear most people may never see the beauty I have been privileged to see and enjoy. Sometimes as I sit here alone...with my cigar…I can visualize a better world. A world where peace and harmony can exist. A world as it was meant to be. For a brief moment, I believe I can almost comprehend the world the Creator had in mind as He was in the process of creating it.

But now the moment is over. As the flame dies I rub my cigar between my palms until only a handful of small fragments remain. With the proper respect I return these fragments back to Nature. The cycle is complete. Nature has given and it has received. The carefully grown leaf has completed the Purpose for which it was created. It has been transformed into a tribute to the very Nature that gave it life.

The Storyteller

It was very flattering for a small boy! Barely ten years old and I am going on a long journey to my uncle's farm to spend the summer working in the olive groves. I will be earning some money for my family that will be needed to get through the winter. Mother would have gone with me, but she was needed at home to care for my sick grandmother and my little sister. "My son", she said softly, Although you are young and small for your years, you are the man of the house. Uncle Jahab needs help. He has agreed to pay you one-half of a man's wages if you will help him. It is a six-day journey, but you will be traveling with others from our village. I ask only that you stay close to the elders and pay heed to their bidding. I have little food to spare, but here are six barley cakes and three fishes. If you eat a barley cake and half a fish each day at the mid-day meal you will have enough food for the journey. It is important that you eat wisely so that the food lasts. Otherwise you will arrive weakened and unable to do a man's work". With that final admonition she kissed me and waved good-bye.

Musings from the Mountaintop

The journey was difficult. The road was hard and dusty, and the other villagers had longer legs. Keeping up with them was more difficult than I had imagined. I amused myself from time to time by looking at the passing clouds. That one looks like old Jacob the merchant. See, there is the large stomach and there, his long nose! And there, a camel! And there a fine chariot! I began to laugh out loud. This seemed to annoy my fellow travelers. "Keep up, boy. We have far to journey and we can not wait for you!" scolded one of the men. His words made me realize that I had fallen fifty paces behind. I ran to close the gap. As I walked I broke off tiny pieces of barley cake, and now and then a bit of fish. At mealtime I realized I had already eaten most of a barley cake and nearly an entire fish. Mother had told me that to make the food last for the entire journey I should eat just one barley and half a fish each day. As I finished the barley cake my fears and loneliness took over. I hid my face and sobbed softly. I have eaten too much of my provisions. I have no money to buy more. If I do not make the food last I will become weak. What if I fall behind the others and am devoured by a wild beast? The long journey took its toll and my fears gave way to a deep sleep.

Just before sunrise I was awakened by one of the men with a nudge from his sandal. "Awake, boy, we are ready to leave". I quickly gathered my belongings and prepared to go. I checked my provisions. It had not been a dream. I had eaten one whole fish. Today I can only eat a barley cake! I must not eat any fish today if they are to last through the journey. Just the thought of not being able to eat any fish today made me even hungrier for the taste of the salty delicacy.

By mid-morning I realized the road was becoming very crowded with people. They were everywhere. They seemed to be heading up the side of a mountain. Our group joined them, finally settling on a grassy slope near the bottom of the hill. It was exciting. There were more people than I had ever seen before. I had always thought the marketplace in our village was crowded, but this multitude was much larger. A man seated nearby said he would wager there were at least five thousand people on that hillside. Surely he was jesting... there can't be that many people in the whole world!

Suddenly the crowd became quiet. Just below us a small group of men had gathered. They seemed to be important. It was like the entire multitude had come just to hear them. As they sat down one of the group stepped forward. He was a bit smaller than the others were, but he seemed to be their leader. His face was sad, but kindly looking. His eyes seemed to look right through me...he seemed to look at each person as he spoke. He began to tell stories about a farmer sowing seeds...and the importance of forgiveness...and about helping neighbors in need. The Storyteller was good. Everyone seemed to listen carefully to his words. In no time at all several hours had passed. The position of the sun told me it was well past the hour of the mid-day meal. I realized I was hungry, and again I thought about how I had eaten too much of my food the day before. I remembered that I must take care to make certain my food lasts.

The Storyteller must have gotten hungry, too. He talked to some of his men and they came up the mountainside and walked amongst the people. I decided to have some lunch, so I took out my barley cakes and the remaining fishes. I was deciding if maybe I could just eat one small bite of a fish, when one of the Storyteller's men grabbed my food. He was a huge man with thick, bushy eyebrows. I was frightened, but concern over the loss of my food helped me overcome my fear. I jumped up and grabbed the back of his robe. "Give it back", I shouted as loud as I could. "You took my food! It must last through the journey. Without it I will be too weak to work!" He looked down at me and smiled slightly. He said simply, "Fear not, my son, your food is needed to feed the Master's guests". For some reason his words had a calming effect upon me. At that moment one of our group took me by the shoulders and pulled me back to my seat. "Be still, boy!" he whispered.

By then the big man had taken my food to the Storyteller. He took the food and looked up at the clouds. Just then the crowd began to murmur. I turned to look, but several men in front of me had stood up so I was unable to see what had happened. When they sat down I could see that the Storyteller now had plenty of food! Enough to feed everyone. When my turn came I ate as much as I could hold...I felt they owed it to me. Even after everyone had eaten they had many baskets of food left. With all that food I couldn't understand why they had to take mine. So, as the crowd began to leave...when no one was looking...I crept over to one of the baskets and took enough food to make up for what the man had taken from me. Actually, I took more! I filled my bag with pieces of barley cake and fish. I filled all my pockets as well. Maybe that was wrong, I don't know. But now I had plenty of food for the journey and some to share with others, if they were hungry...like the Storyteller said. That's not wrong, is it?

Anyway the group was walking quickly now, as if to make up for the time we spent listening to the Storyteller. I had to run to keep up with them. I tugged on the sleeve of one of the men. "Who was he?" I asked. The man looked at me for a moment in disbelief. "Don't you know? He was the Nazarene...the King of the Jews!" He smiled as his eyes turned again to the road ahead. I was angry. I am heading to the groves with them to do a man's work, and yet they treat me like a child. They mock me! King, indeed! How could the Storyteller be a king? His cloak was no finer than my own! He had no gold, nor silver! He had no army! He didn't even have a camel...or a single calf. No, he was just a Storyteller...but his stories were really good! But I would really like to know where all that food came from!

I was becoming bored with the journey. The road was hard and dusty. My sandal had a pebble in it. And my only source of amusement, the clouds, had disappeared before the setting sun. I am getting tired. But, as I patted my bulging pockets, I couldn't help but smile. At least now I have plenty of food for the journey...it was a miracle!

Managing Diversity

The most important skill any leader or manager can possess is the ability to continually raise the organization's level of performance. Regardless of the size of the organization it is the key to sustaining long-term growth and prosperity. One of the greatest challenges is keeping your people on the same page. People bring a range of perspectives to the table and an effective leader must learn to channel them in a way that compliments the organizational mission.

Think of it this way. In every organization people view problems and opportunities from completely different perspectives. It is as if they were looking through the opposite ends of a telescope. People who look through in the conventional manner see "problems and opportunities" as being very close at hand. They feel a heightened sense of urgency and the need to take immediate action.

At the same time there are those people who look through the opposite end of the telescope and see the same "problems and opportunities" as off in the distance and far less critical. They feel no sense of urgency and no need to make what they consider to be hasty moves. The result is a difference of opinion, which at times can cause serious conflicts within the organization.

The degree of success you experience as a leader will be in direct proportion to your ability to identify and resolve any conflicts between these contrasting perspectives. The problem is complicated because, in most organizations, 15 to 20% of the people will be at each end of the continuum. One group thrives on being involved in the change process. They will embrace almost any change. They enjoy the prospect of new experiences. At the other end a group of approximately the same size will resist change with equal vigor. They are uncomfortable with change and prefer the status quo.

About 50% of the organization will remain open to change as long as they understand how the change will affect their work. If the change is beneficial to the organization, and doesn't increase the complexity of their work, they will generally be supportive. While this group represents the majority, the other two groups will require most of your attention.

It is important to realize that people do not arbitrarily line up on opposite sides of an issue. And differences in perspective are not rooted in the individual's race, gender, or age. The position they take is based more directly upon their unique personal assessment of their experiences or perceptions resulting from their particular upbringing.

The problems occur because of the time and resources wasted while the people at each end of the continuum lobby for their point of view. This activity can take the form of covert and overt acts. The people lobbying for the change will begin to spend far too much time in meetings to "sell" their point of view. At the same time the other group will resist the change just as aggressively by dragging their feet and retarding the implementation process. In either case the wasted effort will be costly to any anticipated performance improvement.

As the leader you need to understand both perspectives so that you can make the most effective decision. But once the decision is made your effort must be directed toward making certain both parties get behind the implementation process.

As with most organizational problems, an effective vision can help minimize the after effects. The vision tends to close the gaps between perspectives and to resolve differences of opinion. While differences of opinion, to some degree will always be a part of organizational life, your ability to utilize them in your decision-making and resolve them early in the implementation process will go a long way toward improving organizational performance.

The Wall of Decisiveness

I was cleaning out an old building that had been in our family for generations. The building was being sold and it became my task to remove several truckloads of accumulated junk from a storage area in the back of the basement. It was there I found an old brass chest. The ancient latch had been sturdy in its day, but with a few taps from a small hammer it reluctantly yielded its contents. Inside was a scroll. As I unfurled and read the scroll a fascinating story unfolded.

* * *

Behold, at the top of a high mountain, at the end of a well-traveled path lies the Wall of Decisiveness. It was so named because it is where all of those who journey there make the most important decisions of their lives. It is there that decisions are made that mold futures and guide destinies. I write this scroll in the hope that all who read it will recognize the importance of these decisions and that they will ponder mightily their personal decisions before they make commitments that will forever bind them to their futures.

It is as though it was yesterday that I made the journey to the Wall with my father Haggi, the wise man. It was he who explained the function of the Wall and how it affected the lives of men. At the base of the Wall were three doors of solid oak with fixtures of gleaming brass. Each door was labeled in letters of gold and bore a large golden plaque that spelled out the commitment that must be made by all who entered. The first door was labeled **VOCATION**, and the tablet promised that each person who entered this door would achieve great success in whatever profession they chose, be it in the arts, commerce, politics, law, academics, etc. That they would achieve untold fame and fortune...that they would reach the pinnacle in that field. However, if they entered the door, in exchange for their success, they would forfeit any success in family life and they would be unable to experience a rewarding spiritual life.

It has been chronicled that all those who passed through that portal did indeed achieve tremendous success in whatever field of endeavor they selected. They prospered...they were revered by their peers...they were recognized far and wide as leaders in their fields...they achieved unparalleled status. As promised they became great doctors, famous politicians, athletes, lawyers, professors, and businessmen and women. But none of them ever became successful parents...none of them became spiritual leaders. In fact they did not seem to have any empathy for persons not affiliated with their chosen field. None were ever totally happy, nor completely satisfied.

The second door was labeled **FAMILY LIFE**. The tablet promised that each person who passed through that portal would find the perfect spouse and together they would enjoy a fulfilling family life. They would have healthy, gifted children who would be of continuous joy and pleasure to them. They would live long and rich lives. But, they would only earn sufficient wages to provide for their basic needs...food...clothing...shelter... education. But not a penny more. And beyond the warmth of the loving family they would feel nothing in the way of a spiritual life. Compassion and love for their fellow men would all be a void...an unseen, unknown void.

It is written that all this came to pass for those who chose this door. They were happy within the confines of their families. They became wonderful parents. They doted on their progeny, supportive of their activities, encouraged their talents and gifts, and nurtured their every desire. As parents they were without equal, but there were never any funds for anything beyond the necessities and no time for any activities outside of family life. No time for church... or good deeds...no time for helping fellow men in need...no spiritual growth. They, too, enjoyed great joy in their selection, but none were ever totally happy, nor completely satisfied.

The third door was labeled **SPIRITUAL LIFE**. The tablet promised that each person crossing the threshold would find a full, rich spiritual life, a close and personal relationship with their God.

By selecting this option they would be able to devote their lives to doing good for others...to enriching the lives of others... healing their souls and addressing their spiritual needs. They would experience an immensely rewarding life with an abundance of opportunity to do well. But they would only earn enough to provide for the barest of essentials...food, clothing, and a meager shelter. They would have no family life to speak of...if there was a family at all, there would be prolonged periods of separation with little or no contact.

Those who chose this portal were exceptionally blessed with gifts of a spiritual nature. They were given many opportunities to perform good deeds. They continually spoke words of comfort to all that passed by, and helped everyone in need. They mended broken spirits and healed wounded souls, as promised. They were indeed one with their God. Over the centuries all mankind has encountered at least one of these people knowingly, or unknowingly. However, quite often their message went unheeded, even by those who sought them out. While they were able to accomplish much, there was always much more to do. With this in mind, none of these people were ever totally happy, or completely satisfied.

After I had spent considerable time pondering these options, old Haggi, looked down at me and asked, "And so, my son, which door would you choose?" My father had taken me many places and had shown me many things. When he asked a question I knew he wanted a carefully thought out response. Over the years I had learned to think carefully before answering...to look beyond the obvious...

and to make my observations complete and detailed. It was then I noticed something strange. Many footprints led <u>away</u> from the Wall! They led back down the steep mountain path. Many of the people who had made the strenuous journey had left <u>without</u> making this very important life-shaping decision!

I thought about all that was before me for a time, and then I spoke. "Great Haggi, each portal offers a guarantee of success in one of three important areas. Any person who journeys here can select a life of assured success in any one of the areas— VOCATION...FAMILY LIFE...or SPIRITUAL LIFE".

"So it is written, my son", said Haggi.

"But yet many who made the journey have left without selecting one of the doors! They have chosen to return from whence they came rather than enter one of the doors!"

Haggi smiled slightly, "And...?"

"It would seem that success in one area, to the exclusion of the other two, was not acceptable to most of the people who have come here! The majority of the people must have felt the price was too high...that success in one area meant they had to give up too much. Perhaps they desire more balance in their lives".

"And how would they achieve this balance, my son"?

"I believe that true happiness will only come to he who can devote a portion of his life to <u>each</u> of the three areas...an equal amount of a lifetime should be devoted to the chosen vocation, the family, and to the pursuit of a spiritual life".

"And how might this be accomplished? How can a person be certain they are devoting an equal amount of their life to each area?" asked the wise man.

I thought for a moment before I answered. I did not want to disappoint my father, who obviously was quite concerned about my answer. "Each man must divide his life into three compartments... like the three doors before us. When he is engaged in earning his daily bread he should give it his full attention and put his family and his spiritual life aside. When he is with his family he should not be concerned with matters concerning his vocation. And when he is engaged in matters of the spirit nothing should distract him from his devotion to his God. In this way each would receive an equal portion of his time and his life's energies...he would benefit from a balance in all three areas...each getting his full attention at the most appropriate time...each treated as an equal in importance".

"You are wise beyond your years, my son. I am proud of you. As you have so ably noted, most people have difficulty selecting one door to the exclusion of the others. Instinctively most people recognize that the choice of one over the others will result in an imbalance, and a void will result in some phase of their lives. Therefore, they decide <u>not</u> to make a decision and they journey back down the mountain. This, too, is a <u>decision</u>! You were also wise to recognize that true happiness can only result from a life that devotes equal time to each of these three areas. But to create a balance by dividing a lifetime of activity into three separate compartments is also difficult. It would involve many complex decisions throughout each day as to which compartment you were in and to whom you should be devoting your attention".

Haggi paused to make certain I understood each nuance of his words. I nodded to indicate I understood.

"There is a better way, my son. All mankind can achieve true happiness <u>and</u> ultimate success by simply engaging in all three areas <u>simultaneously</u>! When involved in matters related to the vocation one must recognize that they should conduct their affairs as they would if dealing with members of their own family. They should apply the rules set forth by their God. They should treat others as they desire to be treated. They would also work harder when they remember they are working to provide a better life for their families.

"When with their families they should think about what a family is—a spouse to be cherished and loved...children who in reality are innocent souls entrusted to the parents for a brief time by a loving God. When the Spiritual Life is entwined with Family Life and Vocation it becomes even more meaningful. It provides a balance in times of trial and discontent. It provides a sense of calm in a raging storm. It provides the focus...the guidance system for all other activities. You see, my son, for total happiness and complete satisfaction the three must be combined and experienced simultaneously. Only then can a lifetime be meaningful and fulfilling. All life's energies should be devoted toward successfully combining the three into one."

With these words we turned from the Wall and climbed down the mountain. I began my life anew, applying the principles as suggested by Haggi. And now, having experienced a full rich life, I prepare this scroll to bear testament to the words of Haggi...that all who read it and heed it's words may benefit as I have.

>Your faithful servant,

>Abban, Son of Haggi

* * *

It has been over sixty years since I found the scroll. Each day I have faithfully applied the principles to my life, as have my children and their children. In return the blessings we have received have been multiplied many times over. And so, in the autumn of my days, I pass the words of old Haggi on to you with a prayer that you use them so that you, too, might share in the great abundance of life.

Conversation with a Jackrabbit

A few days ago I was sitting in one of my favorite writing spots up on the mountaintop. I had just finished my lunch and was wrapping up an article when I spotted a jackrabbit about twenty or so feet to my right. I watched it for a time, taking care not to make any quick moves that might frighten it. After a time I went back to my writing. When I looked up again he had moved to within ten feet of my perch. I admit I was a bit startled. I've never gotten that close to a jackrabbit since I nearly stepped on one a few years back.

"You're sure a skinny little fellow", I said. "If I had known you were stopping by I would have saved you some of my sandwich. I've got nothing left except a couple pieces of beef jerky. I hardly think you would be interested in that."

"Thanks, but I'm not hungry", he replied.

I almost fell over! Have I been out in the sun too long?

"I could have sworn you just spoke to me…you did speak, didn't you?"

"Of course", he said defensively. "And I'm not skinnier than any other jackrabbit. We all tend to be on the lean side".

"I'm sorry, I didn't mean to be critical".

"No offense taken. None of us will ever get too big on the food we are able to scrounge up around here. Besides we can't afford to…we're on the bottom of the food chain, you know. We lose any speed and we're fair game for every thing else".

"I suppose so." I thought for a moment. "I guess that's why I don't see too many of you anymore."

"That's because there aren't many of us around any more. Between the land developers and the farmers and ranchers there isn't much room for us. If it wasn't for our speed and our ability to hide we would all be gone." He laughed dryly.

"I thought you were considered an endangered species."

"We are, according to your government, but that's a big joke."

"How so?"

"They put us on the list, but they failed to set aside any land to protect us. We have no place of our own…no sanctuary." He paused. "Think of the irony of this, the buffalo is as big as any animal around. They don't have to run and hide from every hungry coyote or eagle that happens to be in the area. And yet they are protected. They have land set aside for them. There are laws to protect them. Sure some of them are raised for meat and their hides, but most are off limits for all intents and purposes. But us little guys are left to our own devices. We have to depend upon our speed and our wits to find our food and to avoid being killed by every other animal. Every rancher wants to kill us because we eat the same food as his or her precious cattle. Farmers begrudge us what little food we might forage from their land. Anybody with a gun or a bow and arrow can hunt us down for our fur and for what little meat we can provide. Its unfair!"

"I never realized you had it so tough."

"That's not the half of it...our young don't have a chance. From the time they are born, someone or something is after them. During the day they can't go out to play. Even the snakes come after them. The big birds can see us even in the dark. Our eyesight is no match for theirs."

"You need to speak up for your rights."

"Are you kidding? If people knew we could talk they would want us as pets! Every family would want one of us. Why we would make much better pets than any dog or cat."

"You've got a point there." I thought for a moment. "You know, you need some group to speak for you."

"A group?"

"Yeah, like a lobby or something. Like the SPCA that represents the rights of animals...or PETA...some group that will take your case to the public. So that everyone is aware of your plight."

"That's why I've come to you."

"What?"

"You're a writer, aren't you?"

"Well yeah, I guess so."

"I mean we see you up here writing all the time. Why can't you write something about us?"

"What would I say?"

He looked at me in disbelief. "Haven't you been listening to me? Have I been wasting my breath for the past hour? I mean we took a big chance with you. Everyone else we've tried to talk to ran away. They thought they are going insane. If you don't speak up for us it may be generations before we open up to another human being. By then it might be too late. We might have disappeared completely. There will still be plenty of buffalo…but no jackrabbits! I can't help but feel the world would be a better place with at least a few of us jackrabbits around."

"You are right. I'll see what I can do. In the meantime I have enjoyed talking with you. I hope you will come by once in awhile to say 'hello'."

"I promise I'll do that…thanks for caring."

With that he hopped out of sight.

And so, as promised, I am passing on his message to you. They have got a tough life. The next time you see a jackrabbit take a few minutes. Tell them you understand. Tell them you care. You will find they are interesting folks. And…you might make a new friend.

Living Life in a Fishbowl

Immanual Kant, the highly regarded German philosopher, contributed greatly to our present day understanding of moral law and ethical living. His Categorical Imperative presented the theory that there is a single moral obligation that establishes the basics for all other moral obligations. It was Kant's belief that we have an obligation to live our lives as though the whole world is watching us, and that we have that obligation regardless of whether or not we accept the premise.

Even if we are inclined to believe that whatever we do…however we choose to live our lives…is no one else's business, the world is still watching. While legally speaking this may be true, it may not be from a moral standpoint.

Obviously, as parents, we have an obligation to set a good example. As a parent, as a member of society, every day on every news broadcast we see examples of people who ignore the Imperative. Top executives rob their customers, investors, and even their employees. In contemporary society, if they have enough power and money, they can probably beat the rap. Even some of those we look up to as spiritual leaders snub our moral and ethical standards.

But my purpose is not to dwell on the negative consequences of ignoring the Imperative. Rather I would like to stress the positive aspects of accepting and acknowledging the moral and ethical laws. The more we <u>live</u> these laws the more we contribute to these laws being universally accepted. It is like a rippling effect. As we concentrate on living a 'good' life we set an example for others to follow, and thus create an ongoing wave of acceptance that will in time envelope the entire universe. One person, YOU, can accomplish all of this.

Live your life…each and every day…as if the entire universe is watching you. Concentrate first on your family. The Bible says, "Train up a child in the way they should grow, and when they are grown they will not depart from it." It has also been written that, "As the twig is bent, so grows the tree." Your children watch you every day. Live a moral life and they will follow. Live a hypocritical life and they will turn away from you and embrace the opposite of what you say you stand for.

In the marketplace set a good example by engaging in ethical practices. In the short term a few may take advantage of you, but in the end you will have a profound influence of over those who follow in your footsteps. One of the long-range benefits of living the Imperative is that the people the Universe places in your pathway will be drawn to you. You see, as we go through life, many people have been placed along the way to help us to the next level. It is like the Zen philosophy that assures us that "When the student is ready, the teacher will come."

Most of the time people don't sit for long periods of time staring into a fishbowl. They may look into it for a time, but mostly the observations are passing glances…mere glimpses of what is going on within. And so it is with your life. Nobody is going to watch you every minute of every day…unless of course you are incarcerated. Most likely the public will only make passing glances in your direction…short observations…mere snippets of an understanding of who you are and what you stand for. The problem is you often don't know <u>who</u> is watching and <u>when</u> they are watching. So it behooves each of us to make an attempt to live each moment, of each passing day, as if the entire world was looking into our fishbowl. We should set a good example each day so that regardless of who might be watching they will observe a pattern of living worthy of emulating.

The Cookie Lady

The cookie lady is gone.

She had been widowed for over six years. She rarely missed serving dinner at the grange hall...or at the church...or at the high school alumni fundraisers. Not a pretty woman, by societies' standards. Her beauty came from deep within. She spent much of her free time sewing and crocheting. Every member of her extended family has at least one hand-made afghan and a complete assortment of doilies and placemats.

But she was best known for her cookies and candies. By early October she was assembling ingredients. Sugar, flour, chocolate, nuts, candied cherries, shredded coconut, Ritz crackers, etc., were all purchased in large quantities and stored in every corner of her house. By the first of November she would begin to bake the wide assortment of goodies. Often she would commandeer her daughters and granddaughters into spending entire weekends baking in her modest kitchen, cutting, stirring, assembling, and baking.

Then, as Christmas approached, she would begin distribution. Everyone got a large box of his or her personal favorites. I don't think I ever knew the names of most of them. One was made from Ritz crackers and coated with chocolate; "buckeyes" were made from balls of peanut butter covered with chocolate. Peanut brittle was my favorite. Every year, like clockwork, came my bag of peanut brittle along with a large assortment of other cookies and candies.

I had a strange relationship with the cookie lady. We talked many times over the years. She would call me...I would call her. She never had too much to say—at least of any great significance...and neither did I. She would call to tell me if someone got married, or died. She offered support in times of trouble...shared a joy or two, now and then, but we never got real close. She wasn't too big on hugging, or displays of affection...or maybe it was me who wasn't. Anyway, she never was one to allow you to get a swelled head. If you called to brag about some accomplishment she would say "Uh huh.", and change the subject. She was like that with all her children... and grandchildren...and great-grandchildren. Many times they felt slighted...but that was just her way. On only one or two occasions do I ever remember her saying she loved anyone, me included. It just wasn't her nature to be gushy or effusive. And yet, in her own way she was able to communicate what could not be said directly.

My last remembrance of the cookie lady will be the big smile and the wave of her hand as they wheeled her into the operating room. With no warning, the cookie lady left us a few hours later.

At her funeral hundreds of people came by to pay their respects. Each person remarked about how they would miss her cookies...or how they would miss seeing her at the church dinners...or how they would miss hearing her, with glowing pride, talk at length about something her children...or grandchildren...or her great-grandchildren had done.

The cookie lady is gone...and I miss her very much...she had been my mother for over fifty years!

The Gift of Spirituality

I am constantly aware of the tension some people experience when they feel someone is 'preaching' to them. They become defensive when religion enters the conversation. Whenever I am before an audience, and my presentation deals with some aspect of spirituality, I make a distinction between 'religion' and 'spirituality'. Religion is when people go to church and think about fishing...Spirituality is when people go fishing, and think about God.

Another favorite of mine is the sentiment that...

> "Religion is for people who fear Hell... Spirituality is for people who have <u>been</u> there."

Over the centuries great armies have fought long and destructive wars in the name of religion. Most of the armed conflicts around the world today are because neighbors are willing to kill, or be killed, in the name of their religious beliefs. Their children grow up believing that the religion of their fathers is the only <u>true</u> religion. They are taught that their religious beliefs tolerate, or even worse, encourage the killing of another person based solely on their religious persuasion.

Parents defend the practice because it was what they were taught...the way they were brought up. So the practice continues, generation after generation. For some peoples this has gone on for thousands and thousands of years.

On the other hand, no wars have ever been fought over 'spirituality'. Few lives are ever snuffed out because of a person's spirituality. At worst the person of spirit may be branded a zealot or 'weirdo'. But rarely are they killed.

Why? Why are people of spirit less likely to experience the anger and wrath heaped upon practitioners of one religious ideology by the followers of another? For the most part spirituality is less threatening. Conversations about matters of the spirit are more likely to bring out the <u>similarities</u> in the various religions, rather than the perceived differences.

Spirituality, as it applies to the individual, is especially important. It can be the foundation for a value system that will positively influence life choices at each fork in the road. Spirituality is tolerant. It doesn't take issue with the beliefs of others. Spirituality goes beyond religion. It is non-judgmental. The best test of one's spirituality is the ability to accept other people as they are, without making judgements as to their acceptability to the Creator. You see the omnipotent Creator knows the individual far better than we will ever know him or her. This is true even for our own flesh and blood. He alone knows whether or not they are headed in the right direction. There are times when a person must fall from grace before they can experience their spirituality firsthand. To interfere with this process would place us in a position of working at cross-purposes with the Creator. Not a good idea!

Therefore the spiritual person will only attempt to encourage another person. However, they should provide guidance and direction <u>only</u> when the other person expressly asks for it.

Spirituality is neutral. It is not the sole property of any one particular religious group. At the same time it is part of <u>every</u> belief system. Every belief system, that is, that doesn't preach violence and hatred toward others. People who hate others because of their race or creed would find it difficult to be spiritual in any true sense of the word. The very purpose of spirituality is to help provide solace to a person who is searching for guidance and assistance. To attempt to provide help when it is unwanted or unwarranted is meddling.

A true person of spirit goes through life alert to the possibilities it provides. They do not seek to create opportunities to expound on their personal beliefs. Evangelizing where it is unwanted is likely to do more harm than good. Knowing how to use spirituality is just as important as the gift itself.

So then, is spirituality a gift for a special few...a group selected by the Creator to dispense love and goodwill to the populace just at the precise moment they need it? Is it a divine right given at birth? Is it the sole property of a particular spiritual persuasion...a specific race, or people?

I don't think so. It is my belief that the seeds of spirituality are in each of us. Even the worst among us...the base...the corrupt and evil...have the same seeds. We each have the potential to be a source of spirituality. The seeds are present, but only those who take the time to feed and nurture others will ever experience a harvest.

How do you nurture your spirituality seeds? How can a person develop the gift of spirituality? Well, it is not easy. It requires patience and a deep, abiding concern for others...**all** others. To develop your gift for spirituality you must care equally for all people. And once you pick up the mantle of spirituality, it becomes a full time vocation. You can't just put it down when it is inconvenient, and pick it up again when you are suddenly overwhelmed by a sense of benevolence. Anyone can do that. When you commit to becoming a person of spirit every facet of your existence will be altered. You will become a different person...you will be changed forever. And you can never go back to the person you once were without experiencing a great emptiness in your very being. An emptiness that can never be abated until you once again lift the mantle and return to the person you chose to be. You see, the gift of spirituality is less a 'gift' than it is a deliberate life choice...a **special** life choice, but a choice nonetheless.

Everyone has the seeds...many may attempt to nurture them... but only a few will persist long enough to reap the harvest. The seeds are free, but the effort to plant and harvest them is considerable. However, the rewards of the harvest are incalculable.

snipet views

ATT-I-TUDES…or attitudes?

Maybe I'm a bit slower than most folks in this particular arena, but I recently have become increasingly aware of people with ATT-I-TUDE. You know who I mean…the people who cut you off in traffic…the professional athletes who strut and do those moronic dances whenever they perform a miniscule task for which they are paid a king's ransom…the people who cut into lines (any lines)…and it goes on and on.

I guess what made me think about all this was an incident that occurred a few months back. I was shopping in a large grocery store when a lady banged into me with her a shopping cart. She was looking in a different direction and plowed into me at full speed. For awhile I actually thought my leg was broken. Believe me, I'm not exaggerating one bit, this lady was nearly as large as a full-grown gorilla…with a disposition to match. She actually asked…no <u>demanded</u>…an apology from <u>me</u>! I think she would have attacked me if the security guards had not just returned from their lunch break. As they escorted her forcibly from the store she continued her unending stream of profane epithets. At that point another lady walked over to me and said softly, "Don't mind her...she's got an ATT-I-TUDE!" I couldn't help but ask, "Why?" The lady shrugged and walked away. I thought of the quote attributed to Demosthenes:

"Nothing is easier than self-deceit."

Or this from an anonymous source:

"Conceit is an unusual disease; it makes everyone sick but the one who has it."

I wonder what makes some people feel entitled to subject the rest of us to their ATT-I-TUDE. When I pay good money to go see a sports event, what makes some of the athletes feel I want to watch their idiotic posturing. Having spent some time in Washington, DC, I have seen countless numbers of drivers exercising their 'me-me-me' ATT-I-TUDE as they recklessly drive in traffic. Don't tell me the drivers are just as bad in LA or New York, or in Pittsburgh, or in any other major city in this country. Okay, maybe they are, but let get on with my point.

Understand that most of my public appearances over the last thirty odd years have dealt with some aspect of how individuals can improve their lives, personal as well as professional, by better understanding their attitudes. Attitudes...not ATT-I-TUDES!

First of all it is important to note the center of 'ATT-I-TUDE' is always "I". People with ATT-I-TUDE generally think of no one but themselves. Their ego is all that matters to them. It is the epicenter of their entire existence. Now there is nothing wrong with a little bit of ego. Everyone needs to have some sense of their personal value, but it should be based on something tangible…something other than just the individual's over inflated personal evaluation of their value. On the other hand the person with a balanced set of attitudes most likely has a more realistic sense of 'self' as it applies to the people around them…they have a greater sense of community. Writer Marianne Williamson writes:

"As we let our own light shine, we unconsciously give other people permission to do the same."

One of the leading contributors to this compulsion to express ATT-I-TUDE seems to be a severe lack of self-esteem…which in turn is major contributor to the increase in violence and abuse. Overcoming low self-esteem is not easy. For many people it has its roots in childhood, when some one close to the individual, often a parent, sowed negative seeds of self-doubt in the mind of the individual. This often leads to self-limiting doubts and can progress to self-loathing, which can result in serious repercussions.

Business executive Lee Iacocca wrote:

> "The greatest discovery of my generation is that human beings can alter their lives by altering their attitudes of mind."

The individual must first learn to overcome these self-limiting feelings before they can move on to recognizing and accepting their real contributions. Confucius said:

> "To put the world right in order, we must first put the nation in order; to put the nation in order we must first put the family in order; to put the family in order we must first cultivate our personal life; we must first set our hearts right."

If there was ever a person on the face of this earth that would have had the right to display an ATT-I-TUDE it would have been Mother Teresa. She fed millions of hungry people for many years with little or no thought about her own needs. It is difficult for me to think about Mother Teresa without thinking about an incident that I understand occurred a few years before her death. A large luncheon was planned to celebrate a special award that was being presented to her. The man selected to introduce her gave a long, detailed account of her life and all of her many accomplishments. When he finished he took a deep breath and said, "Ladies and gentlemen, may I present…Mother Teresa!"

The audience collectively leaped to its feet and applauded and cheered loudly. The diminutive guest of honor walked slowly to the podium and mounted the steps placed there so that she could be seen. As the audience continued to applaud she raised a thin hand to ask for quiet. When the audience took their seats she said humbly:

"I am but a pencil in the hand of a writing God!"

Imagine that, she had accomplished so much for so long, and yet she saw herself as a mere tool in the hand of her God! She is a perfect example of a person displaying 'attitude'…an attitude with <u>others</u> at the center. Contrast this to the people with ATT-I-TUDE… the prancing athletes…the thoughtless drivers…the loud, profane bully in the grocery store…and so on. I can't help but believe that the people who put others at the center of their attitudes will be remembered long after the people with ATT-I-TUDE have slipped from our memories.

The Eyes Have It

For years I guess I have assumed that I was the only person with an interest…no, more like a fascination, with eyes. I believe that by looking into another person's eyes you can determine whether or not they were telling the truth. One person wrote:

> **"My eyes are an ocean in which my dreams are reflected".**

I began to realize that much more information could be gleaned when you take the time to look intently into a person's eyes. I also found that any number of people share my interest. Consider this:

> **"I have looked into your eyes with my eyes. I have put my heart next to yours."**
> Pope John XXIII

What a beautiful thought! Imagine the joy of being able to look into a person's eyes and have the ability to feel such a deep kinship that you could literally place your heart next to the heart of another. Can you imagine anything so special...so symbolic? An old Yiddish proverb says:

"The eyes are the mirror of the soul."

Ralph Waldo Emerson put it this way:

"The eyes indicate the antiquity of the soul."

If you believe this is an overstatement, try it out for yourself. The next time you are having a conversation with another person, look directly into their eyes. Try not to be too obvious. Don't stare into their eyes. Don't make them uncomfortable. You don't want to 'creep them out', as the young people are so fond of saying these days. Actually, if you are 'cool' about it, the other person is likely to be quite flattered. They will think you are interested in what they are saying.

In truth, you will probably find that you <u>are</u> more interested because you will begin to realize you are conversing on a different level than ever before. In essence you are practicing the lost art of 'conversation'. But beyond that, you will be gaining a greater insight into the person and developing a better understanding of what makes them tick. You will be 'connecting'. It is what I believe Alfred Adler, the noted Austrian psychiatrist, was referring to when he wrote:

"To see with the eyes of another, to hear with the ears of another, to feel with the heart of another… this seems to me an admissible definition of what we call social feeling."

I can fully appreciate Adler's sentiments. There was a time when I lived in the city when I got away from my habit of looking into people's eyes. I can't say for a certainty why it happened, but I think that it had something to do with the constant crush of people in which I found myself on any given day. Everywhere I went I seemed to be in a crowd. Not like here in the solitude where I can easily be in touch with my thoughts. When surrounded by a horde of complete strangers moving rapidly in all directions I find I have more difficulty focusing on one particular person. Conversations are more difficult…less meaningful. I had lost what Alder referred to as the 'social feeling'.

I found myself becoming more judgmental…more critical…of people I didn't even know. It was some time before I realized the cause of this change in me. As near as I could determine it was because I had lost the sense of 'oneness' I felt when I could look into a person's eyes. In that environment it wasn't easy to correct the problem. My writing suffered. I found it difficult to relate to other people in general. It was only with the people I worked with, or the people who lived in my building that I form any real attachment.

When I realized the source of the problem I made an extra effort to reconnect to people, even strangers, by looking into their eyes. It was difficult at first. I started with clerks in the stores, cab drivers, people seated across from me on the subway…anyone that was in a close proximity to me. It worked. In no time I had regained an improved sense of 'oneness' with other people…even strangers. It was a great feeling. Having that 'social feeling' made me feel better about myself and the people around me. I no longer felt that people in crowds were imposing on my personal space. I felt more at peace with my surroundings.

There are several enormous benefits to taking the time to look into a person's eyes. First of all, it is hard for a person to lie to you when you are looking them directly in the eye. Even people who make a practice of lying will find it difficult try to pull something over on you. There is a special sincerity that passes between two people who can look one another in the eye. Imagine the joy that is shared by both parties when one can look the other, directly in the eye, and say, "I'm sorry." Who could not forgive any act when such honesty and sincerity is expressed?

So the next time you feel at odds with the people around you… even strangers and crowds, try this simple approach. Look into the eyes of the people. I think you will find that the eyes have it.

Discovering Your Inner-Person

One of the greatest secrets of enjoying a full, rich, successful life is the discovery of your Inner-person. Discovering your Inner-person allows you, at any time, to glimpse the <u>real </u>you...the you completely free of anger, discrimination, bias, guilt... you in your purest form. The innocent you. The you that bargained with the Universe for the opportunity to come to Mother Earth and make your unique contributions.

Before you can benefit from the discovery of your Inner-person you must first convince yourself of its existence. If you don't really believe in it, it can't be of value to you. More accurately I should say it is more a process of <u>reconnecting</u> to your Inner-person. In reality you were once closely connected to your Inner-person. Just prior to your birth you knew exactly <u>who</u> you were and <u>why</u> you were. At the moment of your birth things became a bit fuzzy and as your life is set in motion the connection becomes less and less clear. It is up to you to remake the connection if you are to achieve your destiny.

But if you don't really accept the concept of the Inner Person, it can't really help you. So the first step is to find your Inner-person. People who meditate regularly have surely seen their Inner-person on a number of occasions. They have learned the ability to still the mind...to rid their consciousness of all distractions.

When I am here on the mountain I sit alone facing the most serene vista I can find. I close my eyes until I can absorb the peace and silence that is all around me. One by one I push aside each distraction. I push my way past my concerns, my frailties, my worries, guilts, and my faults. I pass by all the wrongs that have been done <u>to</u> me, as well those done <u>by</u> me.

Guilt, like anger, can interfere with progress toward making the reconnection. Excessive remorse for past errors can also be a major distraction. Once you have truly atoned for your mistakes you must brush them aside as well. They, too, should be pushed to the further recesses of your mind. Once atoned for, these acts are less likely to be repeated.

When in the privacy of my home I turn on my miniature water garden and lose myself in the soft gurgling of the waterfall. I turn on my stereo and listen to soft music. I prefer the Native American music of the southwest. Then I follow the same procedure. I push aside all distractions and drift weightlessly toward my Inner-person.

When you find your Inner-person you will see it looks remarkably like you...because it <u>is</u> you. It is the <u>true</u> you. It is you without all the baggage and trappings you associate with yourself.

It may be a more youthful version of you, which you should take as an indication of the need for a new beginning…that the Universe is presenting you with the opportunity to begin again. Like the Phoenix you will have the opportunity to rise from the ashes…to make a fresh new start.

The interpretation, of course, is for you to make. Whether the connection to the Inner-person symbolizes the need for a new beginning, a slight change in direction, or the need to accelerate your present course, the message will be clear to you.

The Inner-person never condones violence or self-destruction. It always represents a message designed to help you grow as a person and to help others grow. Your glimpse of the Inner-person will leave you refreshed and with a clear view of the possibilities before you. It is like a refreshing and cleansing bath in the solitude of a mountain stream.

The greatest benefit of reconnecting to your Inner-person is that it keeps you balanced and focused in the direction of your true Purpose in life. It is your personal compass that always shows you true North as you journey along your earth walk. It will guide you through the maze of daily life. Be comforted by the knowledge that the vision of your Inner-person will always be with you when you face a time of difficulty and uncertainty.

Dealing with Feelings

A newspaper article reported that the results of a study revealed that an increasingly larger number of people had revealed that they wanted to sock a co-worker. Given the apparent escalation of workplace violence, I wasn't too surprised. According to the research, one employee out of six said that in the past year they had wanted to punch a co-worker. The numbers were even higher for people under age 35, especially those working in clerical, office, and sales positions. The survey included 750 workers over the age of 18.

In a similar survey conducted a few years ago 42% of those polled said they were often "at least a little angry" at work. Within a year the number had increased to 49%…nearly half of those polled!

The Marlin Company who publishes and markets motivational, educational and safety materials commissioned the study. Frank Kenna, the company president said, "This is a serious problem for people who manage any of these people. Their ability to recognize and deal with anger and potentially violent behavior is absolutely critical."

I remembered an incident that happened about a year ago at an assembly plant. Someone had scheduled a group of people to meet with me at a time that was apparently too close to the shift change. Only one employee showed up for the meeting—and he was angry. The first words out of his mouth were, "You don't want to talk to me, dude...I hate this _____ place!" Then he added, "Sometimes I want to get my gun and blow my _____ supervisor away!"

I figured since we were both being paid for the time I was going to get him to talk. During the entire interview he never looked at me once, and I remained, "dude". But in the next few minutes he revealed some interesting information. He said his supervisor often cussed him out and treated him like dirt. "Just like my old man! He croaked a few years ago...good riddance. He used to beat on me all the time when I was a kid. No matter how hard I tried to do something to please him, that old _____ never gave me credit for anything. He said I was a waste of good spit!"

Thinking it might be a good time to change the subject I asked what he would like to do if he didn't have to work. His response was quick. "Oh, me and my buddy are gonna take our motorcycles and go out west. We're going live in Arizona or New Mexico. Man, we'll just ride all day long!" Since I was familiar with the area we talked for awhile about that part of the country. His anger faded as he talked about some of the places he had seen on his last visit. He became a different person...a person you could learn to like.

As he left he stuck out his hand. "Nice talking to you, dude!" As he reached the door he turned slowly and said, "You know, this ain't such a bad place to work…I've seen worse!"

The research pointed out that 64% of those surveyed said that at least part of their frustration was because their equipment frequently malfunctioned. These same people expressed dissatisfaction because they felt their co-workers wasted an average of 75 minutes a day on computer games, personal calls and e-mail.

My advice to you as a leader is this—get to know your people. Show them they are important to you and to the organization. My own experience suggests that 50 to 60% of your people do not need direct supervision if their equipment is functioning properly, and they have a steady work flow.

By investing a little of your time getting to know your people, and eliminating the root causes of their dissatisfaction, you will make significant improvements in reducing stress and improving performance. And at the same you will greatly enhance the value of the person.

The Burning Bush

I remember it as if it was yesterday. It was a cold, rainy Sunday afternoon in late November. I had just finished reading **The Covenant**, by James A. Michener, when the phone rang. It was Peggy Heely, the Director of Adult Ministries at our church. Always one to get right to the point she asked if my wife and I would like to go to Malawi for three weeks on a work camp for Habitat For Humanity. When she explained that Malawi was in Central Africa I was stunned. I still had Michener's book in my hands! This is more than a coincidence, I thought, it is an omen. Surely if I made this trip I would find my personal 'burning bush' and God would reveal to me His plan for the rest of my life!

The months passed quickly and in no time at all we arrived in Lilongue, the capital of Malawi. Immediately I began to search for my burning bush. I looked everywhere...across the rolling hills...in the deep lush valleys. I looked into the eyes of every person I met...even the lepers in the marketplace. Nowhere did I see my burning bush. After three weeks I left Africa without seeing a trace of anything that resembled my burning bush...except for one incident. I was helping Robert, a native employed by Habitat, to install windows and doors on a recently completed home. We had barely begun when I heard a strange noise. In the yard of the house next door there was a thin lady tending to her chores. On her back, wrapped in a faded piece of cloth was a tiny baby. The baby was crying...actually it was more like a continuous, ear-piercing scream. I must have glanced out the window several times before Robert spoke. Without looking up from his work he said slowly, "The child is very, very sick".

The screams continued unabated for several hours. Then, slowly, the lady stopped her work and stood erect. She carefully lifted the child from the wrap and with only the slightest hesitation she carried it at arms length to the furthermost corner of the property. There she gently laid the tiny bundle on the bare ground...turned...and without looking back, she returned to her work. The screams continued throughout the day. By late afternoon Robert and I had finished our work and were preparing to return to the Habitat complex several blocks away. As we were leaving I could still hear the screams, but they were softer now...and further apart. I could guess how this story would end. In a day...two at the very most...there would be a brief interment at the lot next to the little neighborhood church. It is a frequent occurrence in this region...I saw at least a dozen services for children in the brief time I was there. But before you judge the mother harshly think about this—the nearest doctor was a full days walk, one way. And there is barely enough money for food, let alone medicine. Maybe the next baby will be healthier...with a better chance to survive.

You know, it has been over a decade since that day, but if I close my eyes I can still see that tiny face...and hear those horrible screams. Maybe <u>that</u> was my burning bush. Maybe it is <u>your</u> burning bush as well. Whether it is in Africa...or Pittsburgh...or central Los Angeles...we <u>are</u> indeed our brother's keeper! We must seek out every opportunity to help our less fortunate brothers and sisters...to feed the hungry...clothe the naked...shelter the homeless.

As the man from Nazareth said so many years ago...

"In as much as ye have done it unto the least of these my brethren, ye have done it unto me."

The Cultivator and The Carpetbagger

*T*wo men came upon the land. Each had a bag slung over his shoulder...each had a dream, and a plan. One man, the Cultivator, carried a crude canvas bag filled with seeds. The other man was known by his colorful bag, made from the finest carpeting... his bag was empty. The Cultivator believed that with a single kernel of his corn he could grow a plant that would bear at harvest at least three ears of corn. By repeating nature's cycle of planting and harvesting, over a period of time, he could grow enough corn to feed the land's entire population.

You see, he believes in the future. He loves and respects the land. He sees every barren field as an opportunity. He knows that where there is a source of food a community will spring up. He knows that with hard work and time he can create abundance...enough to amply take care of his needs and the needs of many who will surely follow in his footsteps. He believes he is entitled to a fair share of this abundance for his toil, but he also recognizes that he has an obligation to others. He knows that others share his toil. Someone prepared the land... someone will water the land...someone will weed and fertilize it. He is only part of the process that creates the abundance. He also knows he has an obligation to help feed others who are not growers...people like the man who made his sandals...and his robe. The man who built his home...and the man who will turn his corn into flour...and still others who will bake his bread.

For those people, and many others with whom he may never trade, or even meet, for that matter, he has this unwritten obligation to do his part...to share in the labor that contributes to the benefit and welfare of all peoples. This is his dream...to work hard so that the process may continue, and that every person who likewise toils at his or her profession can grow and prosper.

And so today...and tomorrow...and the next day he will labor. He will diligently and devoutly plant his seeds...one seed at a time. He may hum a tune as he patiently performs his task. Seeking only a just reward for his work. Honest pay for honest sweat.

The other man, the man with empty bag made of carpet, also sees the promise of the land. He knows it will produce abundance. He too understands the laws that govern the creation of wealth and prosperity. He also understands the obligations one man owes to others of his kind. But his perspective is different. He views these laws only as they apply to the rapid accumulation of great wealth. He feels these laws were created to serve men with the guile and wisdom to take advantage of available opportunities...men like himself. Men *who recognize these opportunities and can exploit them for personal gain. They toil not in any field. They feel toil is for lesser men...men of a lesser capacity. They are not concerned with long-term growth and continuous prosperity...only with the spoils they can gather today. They are not sowers...they are the reapers. They feel they should control the future...that they alone have the wisdom to determine the future for others. His dream is to make a quick fortune. To become known for his wealth...and the power and influence it can purchase. He seeks only to build his fortune without concern for the inconveniences that it might pose for others. He thinks not for the future, for he knows he can always find another opportunity, just over the horizon. He has great confidence in his cunning...he feels he was created for this purpose. Like the Cultivator he sees himself as a creator of wealth. But where the Cultivator is content to build wealth for the long term, the Carpetbagger is driven to amass his fortune...to capture it as he would a bird, to use for his own pleasure and amusement.*

The Cultivator will realize his dream. Though he will never achieve fame nor fortune. Men will never live in awe of his power and influence. They will never know of the sacrifices he has made. Most will not know his name, nor even that he existed. Yet he has created an ongoing source of abundance that will allow others, who follow in his footsteps and make their contributions, to grow and prosper for generations to come.

The Carpetbagger will hold a great banquet to celebrate his newfound wealth. He and his friends will dine heartily on the fruits of the harvest they did not sow. They will sing and dance and make merry. But after the feast they must move on...or starve. For them there is no future on this land...for they have eaten the seed corn. There is nothing left to plant...and there will no crop to harvest next season. But in their hearts they feel no sadness or remorse, for they know there is always another land, and another crop to harvest. Until, of course, they reach the point where there is no fertile land... and there is no crop waiting to be harvested. For them the land will be barren and hold no promise for the future.

With the Cultivator a community is born and flourishes...with the Carpetbagger a community withers...and dies.

The world is well populated by both men. And so my friend I ask you now, which are you...a Cultivator...or a Carpetbagger?

Printed in the United States
62182LVS00002B/1-150